D0961954

SELLING
THE
INVISIBLE

SELLING
THE
INVISIBLE

A Field Guide to Modern Marketing

HARRY BECKWITH

WARNER BOOKS

A Time Warner Company

Warner Books, Inc., 1271 Avenue of the Americas, New York, NY 10020

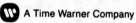 A Time Warner Company

Printed in the United States of America
First Printing: March 1997
10   9   8

Library of Congress Cataloging-in-Publication Data

Beckwith, Harry.
    Selling the invisible : a field guide to modern marketing / Harry
Beckwith.
        p. cm.
    ISBN 0-446-52094-2
    1. Service industries—Marketing. I. Title.
HD9980.5.B425   1997
658.8—dc20   96-16774
                                         CIP

Book design and composition by L&G McRee

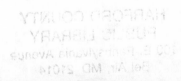

*To Susan,
and miracles*

Contents

Preface **xiii**
Introduction **xv**

GETTING STARTED **1**
  The Greatest Misconception about Service Marketing **3**
  A World on Hold **4**
  The Lake Wobegon Effect: Overestimating Yourself **5**
  Those Cartoons *Aren't* Funny **6**
  Let Your Clients Set Your Standards **7**
  Bad News: You Are Competing with Walt Disney **8**
  The Butterfly Effect **9**
  A Butterfly Named Roger **10**
  To Err Is an Opportunity **12**
  The Ad-Writing Acid Test **13**
  The Crash of Delta Flight 1985–95 **14**
  Getting Better vs. Getting Different **15**
  The First Rule of Marketing Planning **18**
  The *Possible* Service **19**

SURVEYING AND RESEARCH:
  EVEN YOUR BEST FRIENDS WON'T TELL YOU **21**
  Even Your Best Friends Won't Tell You **23**
  But They Will Talk behind Your Back **24**
  Why Survey? **25**
  The Letterman Principle **26**
  Frankly Speaking: Survey by Phone **28**
  The One Question You Should Never Ask **30**
  Focus Groups Don't **31**

MARKETING IS NOT A DEPARTMENT 33
    Marketing Is Not a Department 35
    Marketing Myopia 36
    Tunnel Vision 37
    Start with You and Your Employees 38
    What Color Is Your Company's Parachute? 38
    What Are You Really Selling? 41
    One Thing Most Experts Don't Know 42
    Who Is Your Client? 42
    With Whom Are You Really Competing? 43
    Hit 'Em Where They Ain't 45
    The Adapter's Edge 47
    Study Your Points of Contact 50
    Life Is Like High School 51
    Voted Best Personality 53

PLANNING: THE EIGHTEEN FALLACIES 55
    Fallacy: You Can Know What's Ahead 57
    Fallacy: You Can Know What You Want 60
    Fallacy: Strategy Is King 61
    Fallacy: Build a Better Mousetrap 63
    Fallacy: There'll Be a Perfect Time
       (The Bedrock Fallacy) 64
    Fallacy: Patience Is a Virtue (The Shark Rule) 65
    Fallacy: Think Smart (The Crab Concept) 66
    The Fallacy of Science and Data 67
    The Fallacy of Focus Groups 70
    The Fallacy of Memory 71
    The Fallacy of Experience 72
    The Fallacy of Confidence 73
    Fallacy: Perfection Is Perfection 75
    Fallacy: Failure Is Failure 77
    The Fallacy of Expertise 78
    The Fallacy of Authority 79
    The Fallacy of Common Sense 80
    The Fallacy of Fate 82

Anchors, Warts, and American Express:
    How Prospects Think 85
    Yeah, but I Like It 87
    How Prospects Decide: Choosing the Familiar 89
    How Prospects decide: Using the Most Recent Data 90
    How Prospects Decide: Choosing "Good Enough" 92
    The Anchoring Principle 94
    Last Impressions Last 95
    Risky Business 97
    You Have Nothing to Fear but Your Client's Fear
        Itself 98
    Show Your Warts 99
    Business Is in the Details 100

The More You Say, the Less People Hear:
    Positioning and Focus 101
    Fanatical Focus 103
    The Fear of Positioning 104
    Lesser Logic 105
    Halo Effects 108
    No Two Services Are the Same 109
    Position Is a Passive Noun, Not an Active Verb 111
    Creating Your Positioning Statement 113
    Creating Your Position Statement 114
    How to Narrow the Gap between Your Position
        and Your Positioning Statement 116
    If That Isn't Our Positioning Statement,
        What Is It? 117
    Repositioning Your Competitors 118
    Positioning a Small Service 120
    Focus: What Sears May Have Learned 121
    Focus and the Clinton Campaign 123
    When the Banker's Eyes Blurred: Citicorp's Slip 124
    What Else Positions and Focus Can Do for You 126

UGLY CATS, BOAT SHOES, AND OVERPRICED JEWELRY:
   PRICING 129
   Ugly Cats, Boat Shoes, and Overpriced Jewelry:
      The Sheer Illogic of Pricing 131
   Pricing: The Resistance Principle 132
   Avoiding the Deadly Middle 133
   The Low-Cost Trap 134
   Pricing: A Lesson from Picasso 137
   The Carpenter Corollary to the Picasso Principle 138
   Value Is Not a Position 139

MONOGRAM YOUR SHIRTS, NOT YOUR COMPANY:
   NAMING AND BRANDING 141
   Monogram Your Shirts, Not Your Company 143
   Don't Make Me Laugh 144
   To Stand Out, Stand Out 144
   Tell Me Something I Don't Know 145
   Distinctive Position, Distinctive Name 146
   What's in a Name? 147
   Names: The Information-per-Inch Test 147
   The Cleverness of Federal Express 149
   The Brand Rush 150
   Aren't Brands Dying? 152
   The Warranty of a Brand 153
   The Heart of a Brand 154
   What Brands Do for Sales 155
   Stand by Your Brand 157
   The Four-Hundred-Grand Brand 158
   Brands in a Microwave World 160
   Brands and the Power of the Unusual 161
   Brands and the Baby-sitter 163

HOW TO SAVE $500,000:
   COMMUNICATING AND SELLING 167
   Communicating: A Preface 169
   Fran Lebowitz and Your Greatest Competitor 170
   The Cocktail Party Phenomenon 171

The Grocery List Problem 172
Give Me One Good Reason 173
Your Favorite Songs 174
One Story Beats a Dozen Adjectives 175
Attack the Stereotype 176
Don't Say It, Prove It 177
Build Your Case 178
Tricks Are for Kids 179
The Joke's on You 179
Being Great vs. Being Good 180
Superiority 182
The Clout of Reverse Hype 184
The First Banks Lesson: People Hear What They See 185
Make the Invisible Visible 186
The Orange Test 188
Our Eyes Have It: The Lessons of Chicago's
    Restaurants 189
How to Save Half a Million 191
The Hearsay Rule 192
Metaphorically Speaking: The Black Hole
    Phenomenon 193
The Generative Power of Words: The Gettysburg
    Address 194
A Robe Is Not a Robe 196
Balderdash 197
Improve the Silence 198
What's Your Point? 198
The Vividness Effect 199
Vivid Words 201
The Value of Publicity 202
Advertising Is Publicity 202
Advertising Begets Publicity 203
The Essence of Publicity 205
Inspiration from William F. Buckley 206
Focus on Buying, Not Selling 207
The Most Compelling Selling Message 208
What Blank Eyes Mean 209

Presenting's First Rule: Imitate Dick 209
Mission Statements 211
What a Mission Statement Must Be—and Must Have 212
When to Can a Mission Statement 212
What Really Sells 213

HOLDING ON TO WHAT YOU'VE GOT:
NURTURING AND KEEPING CLIENTS 215
Relationship Accounting 217
The Day After—Why Getting the Business Can Be
    the First Step in Losing It 219
Expectations, Satisfaction, and the Perils of Hype 221
Your Patrons Are Saints 222
Thanks 223
Where Have You Gone, Emily Post? 223
Poised for a Fall 225
Satisfaction and Services 226

QUICK FIXES 231
Manage the Tiny Things 233
One Ring 233
Speed 234
Say P.M., Deliver A.M. 235
Note to Myself 235
Shoot the Message, Not the Messenger:
    The Fastest Way to Improve Your Sales Force 236
Personal Investment 238
The Collision Principle 239

SUMMING UP 241
Recommended Reading for Service Marketers 246

Acknowledgments 251

Preface

You can't see them—so how do you sell them?

That's the problem with services.

I first learned this fourteen years ago when I wrote my first ad for a service. It wasn't a product. So I couldn't show the service roaring along S-curves on Big Sur, draped on Cindy Crawford, or served on fine china. I couldn't show the service doing anything, because services are invisible; services are just promises that somebody will do something.

How do you sell *that*?

Years of wondering and twenty-two years of working as a service and with services—including with four of America's best premier service companies—led to this book.

This book begins with the core problem of service marketing: service quality. It then suggests how to learn what you must improve, with examples of techniques that work. It then moves to service marketing fundamentals: defining what business you *really* are in and what people *really* are buying, positioning your service, understanding prospects and buying behavior, and communicating.

Introduction

Peering through Harvard Business School's catalog of marketing case studies, I discover that only one in four cases involves a service.

Two weeks later I see the newest Fortune 500, which for the first time includes service companies. Sixty percent of the companies are referred to as services, but even that figure understates the role of services in our economy, because many of the manufacturers listed in the Fortune 500 are, on closer inspection, something different. Industrial giant General Electric actually derives 40 percent of its revenues from services, for example. Nike, presumably a running shoe manufacturer, does not make shoes. It only designs, distributes, and markets them. Nike is primarily a service company.

Almost three in four Americans work in service companies. By 2005, eight in ten will. But there is the Harvard Business School catalog, implying something different.

In short, America is a service economy with a product marketing model. But services are not products, and service marketing is not product marketing.

A product is tangible. You can see it and touch it. A service, by contrast, is intangible. In fact, a service does not even exist when you buy one. If you go to a salon, you cannot see, touch, or try out a haircut before you buy it. You order it. Then you get it.

You can use your other senses to evaluate most products, too. Take a new car:

You can admire a car from dozens of angles. You can feel the smooth finish against your palm and the comfort of the leather seats against your back. You can hear the steady rumble of the engine, the faint hum of the electric windows, and that special thud of the car door—for most people, the ultimate test. You buy with your nose, too, seduced by that new-car smell the car makers cleverly sneak in.

You cannot sense much about a service, however. You cannot hear the hum of a tax return being prepared, smell a good divorce attorney, or try on a dry cleaner to see if it flatters you. In most cases, you buy a service touch, taste, feel, smell, *and* sight unseen.

Few services have price tags. You interview a service to redo your kitchen, revise your company's pension plan, or cater your anniversary party. At that moment you probably do not know the cost and fear what it might be. A representative of the service promises to "go back to work up an estimate." At that moment you are not sure you will be able or willing to pay the amount the firm eventually quotes.

As a result, you feel even more uncertain and fearful.

You usually know when a product fails. The stereo stops playing, the clutch stops clutching, the milk tastes terrible. Knowing when a service fails is much harder. Was that good advice from your benefits consultant, or good painting from your house-painter—that is, was it the service you bargained for? Who knows?

Because most product failures are obvious and provable, most products can be warranted. Most services cannot be. As a result, your only recourse for most service failures is either painful negotiation or agonizing litigation.

So you buy a service with no guarantees—and even more uncertainty.

Manufacturers make products using a well-tested and monitored process that ensures consistent quality. Service companies deliver their "product" through a series of acts that rarely can be routinized into a reliable process. No genius has devised a process, for example, for producing consistently good print advertisements.

And it is very hard to manage those limited "processes" through which most services are delivered. Take an advertising example again. An agency's account supervisor goes out on a photo shoot, downs four banana daiquiris at the hotel bar afterward, and then tries to lure the female client up to his room. She fires the agency the next afternoon.

What process could possibly have prevented that service failure?

So compared to products, services are loose cannons on deck, capable of pivoting around and blowing up the ship any minute. The poor captain rarely feels in control, and the poor prospect often feels just as worried.

The products we buy are built miles away by people we have never met. So we rarely take product failures personally. The services we use, by contrast, usually are provided by people we have met or at least spoken with. When that person fails to do what she promised, we often take it personally. We ask, "How could you do this *[to me]?*" while the service provider explains, prays, curses, and backpedals furiously—all at the same time.

So as a service marketer—doctor or architect, dry cleaner or accounting firm, broker or house-painter—you face prospects almost shaking with worry, and sensitive to any mistake you might make. That is where your marketing must start: with a clear understanding of that worried soul.

Even if you do not consider yourself a service marketer—if your business is pacemakers, cars, or software, for example—this book applies to you, too. Because chances are you *are* a service marketer—or should be. If you make pacemakers, you know that every time a salesperson defects to a competitive pacemaker company, the doctors served by your salesperson defect, too. Most doctors do not buy pacemakers; they buy that expert pacemaker salesperson who can go into the OR and advise on the device, procedure, and programming. Pacemaker buyers buy a service.

Similarly, many people who buy Saturn automobiles actually buy the intangible services that Saturn offers: no-hassle pricing and vigilant service and maintenance. The car merely gets Saturn into the game; the service makes the sale. Saturn drivers buy a service.

If you sell software, you know that your core product is the software, but that the critical part of your product is all the augmentations: the documentation, toll-free services, publications, upgrades, support, and other services. Your users are buying a service.

Pacemakers, Saturn cars, and software remind us that we live in the age of commodities. New technologies allow manufacturers to copy products with astonishing speed. Product distinctions, the historic centerpiece of product marketing, exist only briefly—and in the prospects' minds, often not at all. Faced with products just like their competitive products, today's "product" marketers typically have two choices: reduce cost or add value.

And what is that added value, almost without exception? Services. Take, as a vivid example, Levi's recent introduction of Personal Pair jeans. With this service, a clerk measures the female customer, then transmits the measurements over the Internet to the cutters, stitchers, and washers who then make the jeans and ship them via FedEx to the buyer. Those old Levi's jeans of the old economy were products; these new Levi's jeans are a service. Virtually everyone forecasting the future says that customized products like Personal Pair jeans will become even more prevalent. And with that, more and more products will become services.

So marketers in this new economy must think like service marketers.

This book is for *all those* service marketers: the 80 percent of us who do not manufacture products—and the other 20 percent who do.

This book reflects how a growing number of successful companies think about marketing, from planning to presentations to publicity. These new marketers focus more on relationships and less on features and benefits; they focus more on reality—and on getting "better reality"—while recognizing the powerful influence of perceptions; they are learning more about the seemingly irrational ways in which people think and act; they recognize the huge influence of tiny things; they understand the near impossibility of being heard, and the growing difficulty of being understood, in our increasingly busy and over-communicated society. Perhaps more than anything else, these marketers recognize that in our increasingly complex world, nothing works more powerfully than simplicity.

The new marketing is more than a way of doing; it is a way of thinking. It begins with an understanding of the distinctive characteristics of services—their invisibility and intangibility—and of the unique nature of service prospects and users—their fear, their limited time, their sometimes illogical ways of making decisions, and their most important drives and needs.

That is why this is not a how-to book, although it contains many concrete suggestions. Instead, this is a how-to-think-about book. Because if you think like these new marketers—if you think more broadly and deeply about services and their prospects—you will figure out dozens of better ways to grow your business.

So let's start.

GETTING STARTED

The Greatest Misconception about Service Marketing

In a free-association test, most people—including most people in business—will equate the word "marketing" with selling and advertising: pushing the goods.

In this popular view, marketing means taking what you have and shoving it down buyers' throats. "We need better marketing" invariably means "We need to get our name out"—with ads, publicity, and maybe some direct mail.

Unfortunately, this focus on getting the word *outside* distracts companies from the *inside*, and from the first rule of service marketing: *The core of service marketing is the service itself.*

I am not suggesting that if you build a better service, the world will beat a path to your door. Many "better services" are foundering because of rotten marketing. Nor am I suggesting that getting the word out is enough. Getting the word out and attracting people to a flawed service is the preferred strategy for killing a service company.

This is what I *am* saying: The first principle of service marketing is Guy Kawasaki's first principle of computer marketing:

Get better reality.

"Better reality" in your service will make marketing easier, cheaper, and more profitable. In fact, some companies have improved their "reality" so much they can almost eliminate the "getting the word out" part of their marketing plans.

The first step in service marketing is your service.

A World on Hold

For years we've heard this is a cold, hard world.

What makes us think that?

It's not our family, friends, or neighbors; we get this idea from dealing with services.

We get it from calling a public television station in New York, which puts us on hold for six minutes before it tells us—electronically—to call back; all lines are busy. We get it from the credit card company that sends a replacement card three months late. We get it from the Minneapolis printer who promises an estimate by noon Thursday, and doesn't call until the following Monday (my experiences in just the last three weeks).

Will Beckwith, age ten, says it perfectly: *Too often, service sucks.*

Service quality has sunk so low that if no one complains about your service, you shouldn't feel good. Most people have given up complaining.

Why has service gotten so bad?

It is partly because companies cannot show precisely that investing more in improving service—

whether in training, salaries, or increased staffing—will earn them more. To improve their profits, companies squeeze costs by squeezing their service until someone—usually a client—screams.

Think of the times when you have received extraordinary service. How much more did you end up spending with that company? How many people did you tell about your experience? How much did they spend?

No, you cannot get a precise figure, but it is a *huge* figure. And it's all in that company's bank.

First, before you write an ad, rent a list, dash off a press release—<u>fix your service.</u>

The Lake Wobegon Effect: Overestimating Yourself

The Average American thinks he isn't," someone once said. Psychologists have proved it.

We think we're better than we are.

When researchers asked students to rate their ability to get along with others, 60 percent rated themselves in the top 10 percent. Ninety-four percent of university professors say they are doing a better job than their average colleague. Most men think they are good-looking.

Our illusions of superiority are so widespread that

psychologists have come up with a name for it. They call it the Lake Wobegon Effect, after Garrison Keillor's famous radio show sign-off from his fictional hometown, Lake Wobegon, "where the women are strong, the men are good-looking, and all of the children are above average."

Being human, everyone in your company suffers from the Lake Wobegon effect, too. You think you are better than you are—and that your service is better than it is.

Service in this country is so bad that you can offer above average service and still stink. By definition, the odds are that you're average.

Assume your service is bad. It can't hurt, and it will force you to improve.

Those Cartoons *Aren't* Funny

You've seen the Quality, Service, Price, Pick One signs, and the You Want It When? cartoons. (Not surprisingly, it's the worst services that are most likely to display these cartoons.)

When I see these cartoons, which suggest that customers expect too much, I always tell the clerk, "I'm going to talk to a couple other places before I decide."

But I *have* decided. I'm not coming back.

If you decide that you cannot offer quality, speed, and price, you're not trying hard enough.

How can McDonald's deliver spotless rest rooms and world-class french fries in 50 seconds for 79 cents?

Forget the excuses, and remember McDonald's.

Let Your Clients Set Your Standards

In many service businesses, the industry—not the client—defines quality.

Consider advertising, law, and architecture, for example.

In advertising, when most creative people say, "That's a really good ad," they don't mean that the ad might build the client's business. They just mean that it has a good headline, good visual—it's *good.* Neat. Cool.

Lawyers think the same way. They'll say, "That's a *really* good brief." Never mind that the brief was equally effective for the client $5,000 earlier. And never mind that the brief covers an issue that might have been avoided entirely through good lawyering.

Many architects treasure buildings that are enormously inconvenient for the people who work inside. Still, architects call them *great* buildings. *Quality* service produced them.

Ask: *Who is setting your standards—your industry, your ego, or your clients?*

Bad News: You Are Competing with Walt Disney

I stride into a coffee shop one morning, hopeful.

Four people are in line, but I decide I can bear that.

Unfortunately, nothing is in line behind the counter. A server hands Customer One a large decaf. The customer had asked for a small regular. The other server is flirting with Customer Two. It's touching and nostalgic to me, but not entertaining enough to make me overlook the delay.

Four minutes later, I get my large latte.

Twenty years ago, I might have accepted that delay. Twenty years ago, I also accepted rest rooms carpeted with wet paper towels, waiters wearing catsup-stained aprons and chewing Bazooka bubble gum, and ten-day delivery from catalogs.

Then McDonald's came along and raised everyone's standards for rest rooms, better restaurants raised our expectations of waiters, and Federal Express raised our standards for catalog delivery. Those services changed our expectations forever.

Now we expect cleaner rest rooms, faster services, and more attentive waiters.

More people every day have experienced extraordinary service. Many have seen Disney World; they know how clean, friendly, and creative service can be.

They have seen world-class service, and now every service has to accept it. Printers, for one wretched example, cannot expect their customers to tolerate service that meets printing industry standards if those industry standards fall below customers' expectations, which they routinely do. The printers' customers have been to Disney World, and that experience has raised their expectations.

A service that does not jump to meet these rising expectations will have a small revolution and a customer exodus on its hands.

Ignore your industry's benchmarks, and copy Disney's.

The Butterfly Effect

In 1963, meteorologist Edward Lorenz announced a stunning conclusion.

For decades, people had viewed the universe as a large machine in which causes matched effects. People presumed that big causes had big effects, and little causes produced little effects. Lorenz doubted this.

The question posed to Lorenz sounded strange but simple: Could the flap of a butterfly's wings in Singapore affect a hurricane in North Carolina?

After considerable study, Lorenz answered yes.

Lorenz's postulation of what is now called the Butterfly Effect was one of several findings in the last twenty years that reflect the unpredictability of everything: weather, the likely outcome of direct marketing programs, and the distant but often enormous effects of tiny causes.

One group of people was not surprised by Lorenz's discovery, however. Those people had seen the Butterfly Effect at work every day. They were careful observers of service companies—a world where tiny efforts often produce enormous, though sometimes distant, effects.

Remember the Butterfly Effect. Tiny cause, huge effect.

A Butterfly Named Roger

On September 16, 1993, a Minneapolis man remembered that Dayton's suit department had promised they would have his summer-weight jacket repaired and ready by that afternoon.

The executive approached the register and was

quickly met by an energetic dark-haired clerk named Roger Azzam.

"I'm here for the jacket," the executive said.

Three minutes later Azzam returned from Alterations with bad news. "Sorry, not ready." The executive had barely started to complain that his heart was set on getting the jacket when Roger disappeared, shouting, "Be right back!"

Almost as quickly, Roger returned. "They will do it *right now* and have the jacket in five minutes, I *promise*," he said.

The customer reacted as most people would. He was touched. Actually, he was more than touched. The clerk had gone so far out of his way that the customer now felt indebted to him.

While the customer waited, he started walking through three aisles of sports jackets.

He spotted a handsome brown herringbone Hugo Boss jacket with a matching price tag: $575.

Naturally, the story ends with the executive buying the $575 jacket—but not only that. He also had to buy a $110 pair of black slacks and a $55 brown, black, and white–striped tie to match them.

In seconds, a tiny flap of a butterfly's wings— Roger Azzam's five-minute dash up to Alterations— created a $740 sale. Not to mention the value of all the publicity Dayton's is getting here right now for Roger's gesture.

The morning after that sale, the senior buyer in Dayton's men's suits department reviewed the sales figures on his computer screen. "I sold another of those Hugo Boss jackets," he complimented himself, crediting his shrewd buying and understanding of his customers. But Dayton's buyer did not sell the jacket. Roger Azzam did—with a gesture almost as tiny as the flap of a butterfly's wings.

Be a Roger, and hire Rogers. Flap your wings.

To Err Is an Opportunity

Roger Azzam's story has another moral that many service marketers overlook.

Even though effective service marketing starts with outstanding service, outstanding service does *not* mean zero defects. In Roger's case, Dayton's service actually had a gross defect: Dayton's had not delivered when promised. But Dayton's profited more from its mistake than it would have profited from perfect quality and zero defects—at least $740 more.

Dayton's profited because Roger's customer knew that to err is human, and judged Dayton's and Roger by what he did after he noted the error. What do you do after you err? Do you pass the buck or talk fast—both of which fool almost no one and make matters worse? Or do you take the hit and fix the problem in a way that says, "*You* really matter to us, and we will get this right for *you*"?

Ask Roger.

Big mistakes are big opportunities.

The Ad-Writing Acid Test

A quick but revealing story. Ten years ago. The Pillsbury mansion near the Minneapolis Institute of Arts.

Chuck Anderson and I are sitting in his second-floor office admiring the Institute and ignoring Chuck's office walls. Those walls are covered with our ideas for an ad. After two days, our creative director notices the stench and boldly enters Chuck's office.

Then he mumbles and leaves.

The next day he returns. He sees we haven't progressed.

He says something I still remember vividly. "If it's this hard to write the ad, the product is flawed."

It's true. If you cannot write a reasonably good ad for your service—an ad that makes an attractive promise to your prospect—your service needs fixing.

Write an ad for your service. If after a week your best ad is weak, stop working on the ad and start working on your service.

The Crash of Delta Flight 1985–95

In 1981, Tom Peters went *In Search of Excellence* and found Delta Airlines, the masters of customer service.

If you ever flew Delta, you probably agreed with Peters's assessment. Delta people did *flash* the warmest smiles; they made you feel like smiling back.

Delta owned the better service mousetrap and, with Peters's books, the airline now had $500 million in free advertising.

What happened?

Delta continued to master service but flunk marketing. Delta's executives napped while American Airlines introduced its Sabre electronic reservations system. This innovation was so well received that some experts opined that American could shut down its airline, devote its entire business to the Sabre system, and earn more profit than Delta's entire airline operation.

When price wars came, Delta failed to communicate clearly about its discounts. Rather than try to decipher Delta's discounts, many travel agents directed their customers to other airlines.

Delta failed to communicate clearly in advertising, too. Apart from talking about its excellent service, something for which the airline already was well known, Delta's advertising communicated so poorly that it cost more than it made.

Delta failed marketing, and soon Delta was failing, too. Despite a reputation for devotion to its employees, the company was forced to furlough pilots. It cut routes. It laid off more people. Delta appeared to be in free fall.

At this writing, Delta's nose still has not come up.

Delta focused on customer service. It delivered service second to none. Today, that focus has flown Delta to the brink of disaster.

Yes, service is the heart of service marketing. But the heart alone cannot keep a service alive.

Marketing is the brains of service marketing. If the brain fails, the heart soon will fail.

Getting Better vs. Getting Different

The service and "total quality" bandwagons have raced through America's businesses, and millions have jumped aboard.

But the swirling dust from the bandwagons has obscured some riders' view of what makes a service business thrive.

America's great service successes are not the companies that did what others did, but a little better.

They are the companies that decided to do things a whole lot *differently*.

McDonald's did more than refine the classic American drive-in. McDonald's took a radical, meticulously orchestrated, incredibly process-driven approach to delivering good quality at great speed for a remarkably low price.

Federal Express did more than refine mail delivery. It invented a thoroughly radical, logistically brilliant, and remarkably well-executed method for delivering packages over great distances at enormous speeds.

Citicorp did more than refine American banking. It pioneered the use of automated teller machines; became the first bank to aggressively market credit cards—an innovation now widely adopted and taken for granted; became the first company to utilize fully electronic funds transfers and the first to introduce floating rate notes; and perhaps most significantly, essentially invented negotiable certificates of deposit, which quickly became second only to checking account deposits as a source of funds for financial institutions.

And H&R Block, Charles Schwab, money market mutual funds, overnight computer delivery, Hyatt Legal Services, and dozens of other incredibly successful services did not simply improve incrementally on existing ideas. They made radical departures.

Yet despite these great success stories, if you sit in almost any planning session in any business, you quickly recognize that unless some company renegade argues against it, the purpose of that meeting is simple:

"Let's look at what we did last year, and do at least 15 percent better."

Fifteen percent better works fine—for a time. That time comes when another company comes along and does business 100 percent *differently*.

If you are in an industry with good margins, that enterprising company *will* come along, and it will make your nights very long.

It has happened in entire industries that failed to innovate. Banks have ceded their historical dominance of finance to insurance companies, mutual fund managers, pension funds, and credit unions. Architects have surrendered large chunks of their business to project management firms. Lawyers are in peril from new companies that offer alternative dispute resolution at much lower fees. Advertising agencies have been bitten from every direction, including by Hollywood agents.

The erosion in each of these industries started in those planning sessions at which everyone looked around and said, How can we do it 15 percent better?

Don't just think better. Think <u>different</u>.

The First Rule of Marketing Planning

Unless warned otherwise, the people responsible for marketing a service almost always will take up where they left off the last time they thought about marketing.

Everyone will assume that the company is in the right business, basically organized in the right way, and staffed as it should be staffed, give or take a few thorns in everyone's side.

And everyone's focus for marketing for the year immediately will turn to "How do we sell this?"

Instead, everyone should start at ground zero. They should ask, "Is *this* viable anymore? Is *this* what the world wants?"

Have we added capabilities or skills that suggest that we should enlarge our scope, to serve new markets? Should we develop or acquire related skills and capabilities? Or should we narrow our scope, and leverage these specialized skills and services we are developing to prospects looking for those specialties?

Whatever questions you ask, you should consistently follow the first rule of marketing planning:

Always start at zero.

The *Possible* Service

Want a good model for marketing your service in the nineties? Study the evolution of the automobile industry.

The first car met only some minimum standards because that is what products and services do in stage one of any industry. In stage one, *meeting acceptable minimum standards* is the driving force: Get a basic, acceptably reliable product. Buyers accept this minimal product—the first car, the first VCR, and the first fast-food restaurant—because they desire the unique benefits it offers. Buyers will accept with that good some bad—typically, the fact that bugs aren't out and the price is high. In the auto industry's first stage, we had any color so long as it was black and a product that got you there—and nothing more. Stage one in an industry, then, is product-driven. Stage one companies offer their clients the *accepted product*.

In stage two, competitors enter. Differentiation of this core product becomes vital. Enter the marketers. They listen and make the refinements the customers ask for: more colors, an ashtray so that drivers can smoke, and later an AM/FM radio. *Answering customer needs* is the driving force during stage two of an industry. Stage two is market-driven. Stage two companies offer their clients the *desired product*.

Few companies enter stage three. These companies are in the pantheon of the marketing gods—the

Disneys, Federal Expresses, and Lexuses. Disney entered this stage when it created amusement parks that went beyond what customers said they needed—or could have imagined. Stage three is the phase that several car manufacturers entered when they created heated car seats, stereo consoles that slant toward the driver instead of facing the middle, and compact car trunks more spacious than those on many luxury cars. In this stage, clients' expectations and expressed needs no longer drive the market. Surveys asking "How could we improve?" no longer produce useful data; the customers have run out of ideas.

To differentiate itself clearly from the many competitors who are meeting its clients' expressed needs, the stage three company must make a leap; it must surprise the customer. *Surprising the customer* is the driving force in stage three of an industry. Stage three, as a result, is imagination-driven, and a company in this stage offers *the possible service.*

Most services are treading water somewhere in the middle of stage two. Many of those firms—particularly many professional services—are still straddling stage one and two. Every service company must look at stage three; that is where glory, fame, and market share lie.

Create the possible service; don't just create what the market needs or wants. Create what it would love.

SURVEYING AND RESEARCH:
EVEN YOUR BEST FRIENDS WON'T TELL YOU

Even Your Best Friends Won't Tell You

Yesterday, a man with a valuable service called me, and fell on his nose.

He started educating me about marketing. He instructed me that each element in a plan is just "part of the overall marketing mix." He actually repeated this statement three times.

I might be easily insulted, but his pitch made me hope that my clients never needed his service, a service with real value.

That salesman did more than fail to sell me. He lost any chance of *ever* selling me.

Did I tell him his sales pitch was bad?

No, I didn't. It wasn't worth a prolonged discussion. And I was afraid to offend him back.

So how will he pitch his next prospect?

The very same way.

People won't tell you what you're doing wrong.

Your prospects won't tell you.

Clients won't tell you.

Sometimes, even your spouse won't tell you.

So what do you do to improve your service?

Ask.

But They Will Talk behind Your Back

I recently was left speechless after I told a client, "The first step to marketing a service is getting the service right. So find out if you have it right. Survey your clients. *Ask.*"

I wasn't ready for her response:

"I don't want to do that," she said. "I'm afraid to hear what they think."

Actually, it was good that she didn't want to hear, because I didn't want her to send the surveys anyway. I wanted an independent third party to send them.

A basic principle in life applies to surveying clients:

Even your best friends won't tell you. But they will talk behind your back.

Make it so your clients *can* talk behind your back, and that you can learn what they're saying. Have your clients send their completed surveys to a third party. Have the third party assure your clients that they can leave their names out, and that their names won't be revealed. Your clients will give far more candid answers.

Have a third party do your surveys.

Why Survey?

Your customers will appreciate it. They'll see that you are trying to improve your service. (One respondent to a recent survey said, "This survey is a good example of why I use this company. They are always looking for ways to serve me better.")

You can have customers score you in different areas, then publicize your high scores in your marketing materials. It gives credibility to your statements about your service quality.

It gives you an opportunity to sell something or to make an offer.

It keeps contact with your clients.

It lets you learn from your mistakes.

It helps you flag possible problem areas and clients.

It keeps you from coasting.

It keeps you from wondering what you are doing wrong.

It tells you what business you are in, and what people really are buying.

Survey, survey, survey.

The Letterman Principle

How should you conduct a survey—with interviews or written questionnaires?

Skeptical of written surveys, and looking for a vivid illustration of why written surveys often work so poorly, I got lucky one night. I turned on *Letterman.*

David's guests that night included Helen Thomas, a veteran political commentator. After some light banter, Letterman asked Thomas a serious question:

"Who do you like in the ninety-six election?"

Many viewers thought Thomas would say "Bob Dole." Others waited for her surprise prediction that Bill Clinton would rebound and win reelection. But Thomas did not answer "Dole," "Clinton," or even "Quayle." She gave an even more surprising answer:

"I don't like *any* of 'em."

Thomas was not going for laughs. She had misinterpreted Letterman's question—just as Letterman had misunderstood how Thomas would interpret his question. Sports fans knew what Letterman meant. "Who do you *like* in the Super Bowl?" for example, means "Who do you think'll win?" But to many other people, particularly women, "Who do you like?" means something completely different.

Ambiguous words such as "like" fill the air. Random House's dictionary offers twenty-six definitions for "read," for example. But no written survey can clarify every word or use words that need no clarification, and no researcher can accurately interpret each word a person being surveyed writes down.

A good case in point: A research firm recently asked adult homeowners to rank the importance of different characteristics of remodeling services. "Quality" naturally scored very high. But what did "quality" mean to those people answering? Did it mean the level of finish and luster? Quality to the eye—or quality as an experienced craftsman would see it? Quality as how well the finished product would function for its intended purpose? Or did they mean the quality of the customer service—the responsiveness of the contractors and the friendliness of the receptionist?

This survey illustrates the problem with all written surveys. The surveyors interpreted the answers based on what *they* meant by their questions—even though the people answering meant many different things by their answers.

When you conduct written surveys, you cannot correct this problem; too often, you cannot even see it. But when you conduct oral surveys, you can clarify your questions and ask people to clarify their answers.

So whenever you are tempted to conduct a written survey, remember David Letterman and Helen Thomas.

Unless you are confident that you can interpret them, beware of written surveys.

Frankly Speaking:
Survey by Phone

An editor from *Business Week* and another from the *Orlando Sentinel* telephoned me recently for background on stories. After I hung up each time, I was amazed by how frank I had been with two strangers.

I wondered why.

Then I read how Lincoln Caplan got hard-to-get information for *Skadden*, his revealing book about New York's largest law firm. Caplan would call the possible source rather than meet in person. He learned that when the lawyers could not see him, they were more willing to talk openly. The lawyers knew that Caplan would never recognize them if he ever encountered them.

That's why phone surveys usually produce more revealing results than in-person surveys. On the phone, people will open up and reveal the information you need.

When you call to ask for an opinion from someone, it says you value their opinion. When *Business Week* and the *Orlando Sentinel* called, that's what they were telling me; they valued my opinion. Flattered, and anxious to live up to the editors' favorable impressions of me, I told them *everything*.

My chattiness was typical, I knew. When I conducted my first background customer research, I was so amazed by how much time customers spent talking with me that I started recording the lengths of those talks. They averaged twenty-four minutes.

Time after time, oral surveys work better. Why?

For one thing, it's physically easier to talk than write. So people say more in oral surveys than they write on written ones. (My agency's average oral surveys produce five pages of text; our average written surveys produce less than two pages.) Oral surveys produce more information.

An experienced interviewer can be more conversational and relaxed with the subjects and can go outside the script to probe even deeper. All of this helps produce more information.

Typically, 40 percent of people will respond to a written survey. (The response can fall well below that.) In oral surveys, you often can get almost 100 percent response.

An oral interviewer makes a personal contact on your behalf. This shows a greater interest in the person responding, and conveys a stronger service message about your company.

Finally, a person's voice conveys feelings that her written words often obscure. (A perfect example: The president of a national collection agency felt confident his agency was satisfying its clients because he had just read the verbatim written responses of seventy-five clients. I read those responses, and they did seem pretty good. Still dubious, I called the woman who had conducted the interviews and asked, "How do you think this collection agency is doing?" "Awful!" Why then, I asked, didn't the responses *sound* awful? "Well, many *did* sound awful," she answered. "It wasn't *what* the clients said; it was *how* they said it. When you *hear* their words, you can hear their anger and frustration.") Oral surveys more accurately show exactly what the person being interviewed thinks and feels.

For a dozen reasons, conduct oral surveys, not written ones.

The One Question You Should Never Ask

W hat don't you like about the company or the service?"

Don't ask that.

You're asking someone to admit they made a bad decision in choosing that company. People won't do that; people like to look smart.

Never ask "What don't you like?"

Focus Groups Don't

A typical discussion:

"We need some information."

"OK, let's do a focus group."

It's very tempting to summon focus groups. For one thing, the term "focus groups" is clever packaging. A "survey" sounds like something that only gives you the lay of the land. "Focus group," by contrast, sounds like something that gets you zeroed in.

Or so you would think.

But you are selling individuals, not groups. Focus groups tell more about group dynamics than about market dynamics. Control types take over focus group sessions and try to persuade the others. The wise but shy types sit quietly, waiting for the hour to end. People's views get changed and distorted by other people's views.

You're selling individuals. Talk to individuals.

MARKETING IS NOT
A DEPARTMENT

Marketing Is Not a Department

A Twin Cities business-to-business company has excellent service, strong salespeople, award-winning sales collateral, and a problem:

The company believes that sales and marketing are for the sales and marketing people.

As a result, that company is carrying an enormous marketing liability. Their CFO is negligent, unresponsive, and rude. People who deal with the CFO have a tainted view of the company, even though the CFO is the only bad apple they've tasted there.

The CFO cost his company over $50,000 in business last year just from one source of referrals:

Me.

The president of Seasonal Concepts, Albert Schneider, stresses how fragile a service business is: "We can have great talent, products, prices, and advertising. But if that sales clerk at the end of the line fails, everything fails. The buyer doesn't return. And if the buyer suffers a very bad experience, he tells all his friends not to come, either."

Everyone in your company is responsible for marketing your company.

Every failure is likely to be costly.

More than half of all Japanese companies do not even bother to have marketing departments, because they believe that everyone in the company is part of the marketing.

Marketing is not a department. It is your business.

Marketing Myopia

Most executives are too busy ducking falling trees to see the forest.

Tunnel vision became so common that Theodore Levitt coined a now-famous term for it: Marketing Myopia.

It is the inability of people to see the broad scope of their businesses.

My friend Geoffrey Moore, who advises high-tech companies and wrote *Crossing the Chasm* and *Inside the Tornado*, cleverly describes this myopia when he describes working with Silicon Valley companies:

"You walk into the president's office, and chat. When you leave, you notice his fly is down. You say nothing and go on to the director of sales. You notice his fly is down, too.

"Then you go see Joan. You have another good talk. But when you get up to leave, you notice that *Joan's* fly is down, too.

"Well, you go back, write your report, and return to deliver it. You open by saying, 'Ladies and gentlemen, we have a Fly Problem here.'

"Well, everyone is stunned. *How did he figure that out?* they all wonder. It comes off as a brilliant insight.

"So much of what passes for brilliant insight in helping a company is reporting what everyone in that company could see, if only they could still see clearly."

It's hard to see the real scope of your business. Ask for help.

Tunnel Vision

I cannot walk into most companies without being aware of their walls.

The walls seem to do more than keep the cold air out. They seem to block out a clear vision of the world.

When companies discuss their problems, they talk about themselves. It's not ego at work. It's just that people talk about what they know, and what people know is their company.

But what people really need to know—what *you* really need to know—is your customers and prospects.

Get out, climb out, have someone pull you out of the tunnel.

Start with You and Your Employees

Don't open a shop unless you know how to smile," says an old Jewish proverb, and that advice applies to everyone in your company.

The fastest, cheapest, and best way to market your service is through your employees.

Every employee should know that *every* act is a marketing act upon which your success depends.

Review every step—from how your receptionist answers to the message on the bottom of your invoices—and ask what you could do differently to attract and keep more customers.

Every act is a marketing act. Make every employee a marketing person.

What Color Is Your Company's Parachute?

Never mind what business you are in—what are you good at?

Richard Boles, author of *What Color Is Your Parachute?*, recommends that anyone contemplating a new career ask that question.

Every business planning its future should answer that, too: What are you good at?

Few businesses answer that question, because few think to ask it. Instead, virtually every person in every service business is trapped in a box. The box is a mental model, and part of that mental model is the standard operating procedure of the business's industry. So the question "What are we good at?" invariably is answered, "We are good at being [architects, industrial psychologists, coffee shop operators, whatever]."

"We are an architectural firm," the architect says, and she builds everything around that model—from the hierarchy of titles to the office decor.

That box—"We are an architectural firm"—is a trap. It traps you into doing what others do, saying what others say, and offering what others offer. It traps you into being the same instead of finding ways to be different.

But what *are* you good at?

Federal Express asked itself that in the 1980s when it realized it should diversify its portfolio. But what is Federal Express good at? The Federal Express industry mental model would lead you to answer, "They're good at overnight delivery" or "fast package delivery." The model would lead you to answer the question with a mere description of the business.

But Federal Express realized that what it is astonishingly good at—as good, perhaps, as history's great armies—is logistics. Federal Express is brilliant at procuring, distributing, and replacing materials. Recognizing this, the company established a consultancy that advises companies on logistical management.

For years, accounting firms decided they were good at accounting. But Arthur Andersen realized that in becoming skilled at modern accounting, it had become very adept at understanding the information systems that push the numbers through companies. So the firm established what has become a well-regarded information management consulting practice.

For years, most advertising agencies decided they were good at advertising. Since many agencies have recognized that what they are good at is interesting and persuasive communicating, more have expanded their services to include public relations, sales promotion, and even presentation and speech consulting.

Your opportunities for growth often lie outside the confines of your current industry description. In fact, fighting within those confines, particularly in mature industries, can cause you to spill too much of your blood and money.

Your great opportunities are in your answer to that question: What are we good at?

In planning your marketing, don't just think of your business. Think of your skills.

What Are You Really Selling?

People in the fast-food business used to think they were selling food.

Then McDonald's came along and figured out that people weren't buying hamburgers. People were buying an experience.

Burger King's brass were sure that McDonald's was wrong. Knowing they made the flame-broiled hamburgers that more people preferred, Burger King executives decided to take that unique point of difference and pummel McDonald's with it: "We're flame broiled, not fried."

This pummeling accomplished nothing, because McDonald's was right: Fast-food hamburger restaurants are *not* in the hamburger business.

Maybe you think prospects in your industry are looking for hamburgers. Chances are that they want something else. The first company to figure out what that is wins.

Find out what clients are <u>really</u> buying.

One Thing Most Experts Don't Know

Most companies in expert services—such as lawyers, doctors, and accountants—think that their clients are buying expertise. But most prospects for these complex services cannot evaluate expertise; they cannot tell a really good tax return, a clever motion, or a perceptive diagnosis. But they *can* tell if the relationship is good and if phone calls are returned. Clients are experts at knowing if they feel valued.

In most professional services, you are not really selling expertise—because your expertise is assumed, and because your prospect cannot intelligently evaluate your expertise anyway. Instead, you are selling a *relationship*. And in most cases, that is where you need the most work.

If you're selling a service, you're selling a relationship.

Who Is Your Client?

Karl often feels overlooked and insecure.

Sharon has seven cats named after the Seven Dwarfs.

Karl loves Stanford football and his eight-month-old son.

Sharon wishes she had more time.

Karl wishes business could be better.

Sharon wishes she laughed as often as she did when she was twelve.

Karl wishes he felt more connected, to people and to life.

Sharon wishes she knew more about you, and knew she could trust you.

Karl craves one thing above all, as William James once observed. He craves appreciation.

Before you try to satisfy "the client," understand and satisfy the person.

With Whom Are You Really Competing?

Every great business school teaches competitive strategy. Professor Michael Porter became famous by writing good books on the subject, and every good marketing plan includes a section on competition.

It appears that you should study your competitors. But once again, this product-marketing model fails you. Service marketers must look at competition through a wider lens—as The Case of the Consultants Without Competitors suggests.

Asked to help position a corporate consulting firm, I ask: "Who are your competitors? How are they perceived? How should you adapt, change, and attempt to position your company, given your competitors' positions?"

Our discussion of competitors seems odd. Few names come up, and few competitors are well known—and most are regarded like lint.

But if your competitors are so few, so obscure, and so badly regarded, why don't you dominate the market?

Their answer is the one you get in many service markets: My client's market, despite the models in marketing planning books, is not a true competitive market. With a few exceptions, companies are not battling to share *that* market. They are battling to create it: to get prospects to want and use their service—instead of doing nothing or performing the service themselves.

One of a million similar examples: A large food manufacturer is considering using industrial psychologists to help in hiring. The manufacturer's V.P. of personnel is not simply trying to decide whether to use Firm A, B, or C. The prospect is trying to decide whether to use any service at all!

In many cases and in many markets—among real estate consultants, extended warranty providers, public relations firms, telemarketers, collection agencies, interior decorators, fast-food restaurants, income tax services, motivational speakers, and millions more— your prospect faces three options: using your service, doing it themselves, or not doing it at all.

In many cases, then, your biggest competitors are not your competitors. *They are your prospects.*

This means that your strategy—never mind all the textbooks—*cannot* be competitive. If you compete aggressively, and implicitly criticize your competitors, you aggravate your worst problem: the prospect's doubt that anyone in your industry can provide the service and value that the prospect needs.

If you expressly or implicitly question the prospect's option of doing it herself, you criticize the prospect and her judgment. That may be an accurate analysis, but it is bullet-through-your-own-foot sales and marketing.

Your real competitor often is sitting across the table. Plan accordingly.

Hit 'Em Where They Ain't

The best strategy in war is to win without a fight."

Sun Tzu gave that advice centuries ago, and Wal-Mart and the accounting firm of McGladrey & Pullen have heeded this advice and prospered with essentially identical strategies.

Sam Walton's brilliantly profitable strategy for Wal-Mart was to go where no sane competitor like Woolworth or Kmart would dream of: to towns that seemed too small to support a large discount store. In 1962, Sam opened his first store in tiny Rogers, Arkansas. Two years later, he christened his second store in Harrison, Arkansas, population 6,000. He opened six more stores before he finally opened a store outside Arkansas, in little Sikeston, Missouri.

Walton claimed these towns and their surroundings for himself, and his domination in these areas produced the profits that fed Wal-Mart's growth into more and bigger communities. Just thirty years after opening that first store in Rogers, Sam Walton died. He was America's richest man, and his company was America's largest retailer.

(Like many clever strategies, Walton's may have been partly accidental. After moving sixteen times in nineteen years with her husband, Helen Walton wanted nothing to do with cities, and insisted that she and Sam settle in a town with no more than 10,000 people. They chose Bentonville, Arkansas, so Helen could be near her family and Sam could be near the best quail hunting in America.)

This "Go where they ain't" strategy has fueled McGladrey & Pullen, the nation's eighth largest accounting firm. With Big Six accounting firms dominating America's largest cities, McGladrey focused its strategy on being the only national accounting firm in much smaller cities: Des Moines, Cedar Rapids, Greensboro, Madison, Pasadena, Richmond, and Cheyenne, for example. In each of these cities, McGladrey is positioned as the brand-name accounting firm in the area—a powerful position.

The advice "Go where they ain't" is not limited to location. A Pasadena, California, attorney goes where they ain't by marketing himself as a motorcycle accident specialist, leaving other personal injury attorneys to fight for the much larger and far more competitive market of automobile accident victims. Several large advertising agencies avoid competition for the large and ruthlessly competitive consumer products market by specializing in agricultural accounts. Fingerhut went where they ain't by focusing its catalog products exclusively on people with so little disposable income and such ugly credit that no other catalog company thought there could be a market there.

Again, the problem with "competitive strategy" is that it encourages you to frame your market in traditional, competitive terms. This frame anchors you to the same structure, system, and markets as your competitors, when the better strategy is to heed the advice of Sun Tzu, Sam Walton, and the bean counters at McGladrey & Pullen: Win without a fight.

Go where others aren't.

The Adapter's Edge

Drive-in restaurants once contented themselves with waitresses on roller skates, hamburgers that oozed grease, and milk shakes that could hold a spoon stiff for minutes. Then McDonald's came along with technology that upended the industry.

For every service that has deployed technology as a weapon, another has taken it right through its heart. You can find one conspicuous example every day in the *Wall Street Journal:* the New York Stock Exchange.

The personification of the old ways of doing things among gentleman brokerages up and down Wall Street, the Exchange was blindsided in the 1980s by computers. Personal computers made it possible for investors to bypass exchange brokers entirely. Just as significantly, the Exchange failed to adopt computer systems, and once it added them, failed to integrate them. In a world that required more speed, the Exchange's slowness and inefficiency forced many investors elsewhere.

Because it has such a strong brand, many people think the New York Stock Exchange is still a giant. If it is, it is a much smaller one.

(Technology alone did not knock the NYSE from its perch. The Exchange also was hammered by another force that drives service industries: innovations by outsiders, which have included tax shelters, Keogh plans, IRAs, and mutual funds. But technology dealt the Exchange several hard blows.)

Consider America's poor—literally—car rental companies. In 1995, Budget lost over $100 million. A major villain was Budget's lack of a yield management system, which can detect competitors' rates and raise rates whenever demand for cars increases. So each time Hertz or Avis dropped prices, Budget wouldn't learn and respond for days. Throughout the 1990s, car rental companies have seemed more interested in bells and whistles— VCRs in minivans and Avis's ill-fated experiment with electronic maps on dashboards are two prominent examples—than in basic time- and labor-saving technology, such as handheld remote checkout devices and current, basic computers. Not coincidentally, while America's airlines and hotels were combining to earn almost $10 billion in 1995, America's car rental companies were combining to earn absolutely nothing.

In service industry after industry, technology creates the adapter's edge. The adapters become more proficient sooner, work out the bugs, and quickly recognize the benefits of the technology. The adapters learn and turn that learning into a great competitive advantage. They race to the head of the curve while others lag, paying for the mistakes that the adapters already have made and learned from.

Today, dozens of service industries are sleeping, content with how things have always been. The sleepers in those industries are so many fish in a barrel for the smart marketer who recognizes the many ways that technology can be applied to make customer service in that industry better, faster, cheaper, and more reliable.

What does this mean? Every service company should have a director of technology who studies and regularly tells management how new technologies can be used for competitive advantage.

In addition, every internal review of a company's marketing should ask four questions that have not been typical of marketing reviews until now:

In our industry, are we second to none technologically?

Among service industries, and compared with firms of our approximate size, are we second to none technologically?

Are we doing all we need today to be second to none two years from now?

Have we carefully considered innovative ways that new technology can be used to improve our service and grow our business?

Make technology a key part of every marketing plan.

Study Your Points of Contact

To get started, study every point at which your company makes contact with a prospect.

Usually, you find only a few contact points.

Your receptionist. Your business card. Your building/store/office. Your brochure. Your public appearances. A sales call or presentation. Just a few points of contact—the moments that decide whether or not you get the business.

Then, ask: What are we doing to make a *phenomenal* impression at every point?

Don't squander one point of contact. It may be your only one.

The points of contact continue once the person becomes a client. But again, the moments are surprisingly few. A call here and there. A meeting now and then. A few points of contact.

Did you get everything possible from those points of contact? Did the client feel respected, amazed, impressed, delighted?

Study each point of contact. Then improve each one—<u>significantly.</u>

Life Is Like High School

Why do so many people in services, particularly professionals, believe that sheer technical competence ensures success? Odds are, they learned that in college.

College and graduate school teach us that technical competence is all. Whether it is Phi Beta Kappa, Baker Scholars, or Marshall Scholarships, the spoils go to the technically proficient: those who know their subject.

None of these institutions reward the human qualities that tests cannot measure—and this is not to suggest they should. But college graduates learn something: Knowing your stuff is what counts.

This lesson of college conflicts with the lesson we learned immediately before it. Children and teenagers learn to value well-roundedness and traits that are likable. A high school student in the 1960s and 1970s could learn that it was an honor to "make" National Honor Society, but an even greater one to get into Key Club, which stressed citizenship, integrity, and other issues of character.

College, then, seduces us with the notion that real life will be an oasis where sheer talent is what counts. This misleading notion is what actress Meryl Streep was reflecting on when a lucky interviewer got a moment with her.

"I really did think that life would be like college," Streep told the interviewer, "but it isn't. Life is like high school."

Life *is* like high school. Those things that made you popular start mattering again. Hate it, fight it, march in the streets against it, but it is true. The competent and likable solo consultant will attract far more business than the brilliant but socially deficient expert.

In large part, service marketing is a popularity contest.

Voted Best Personality

Meryl Streep's observation shows up again in another phenomenon in service marketing: chemistry.

Time and again, we hear that Doe & Associates failed to get the account because "the chemistry just wasn't there." And time and again, that explanation is accurate.

But what is "chemistry"? And if the principle of business should be "Let the best business win," what does chemistry matter?

When many prospects choose a service firm, they are not buying the firm's credentials, reputation, or industry stature. Instead, like the high schoolers we continue to be throughout our lives, these prospects buy the firm's personality.

"I just liked them."

"I had a good feel about them."

"It just felt like a good fit."

Notice carefully the prospect's choice of verbs: "like," "feel," "felt." The words do not refer to logic and reason; they refer to *feelings*.

Service businesses are about relationships. Relationships are about feelings. In good ones, the feelings are good; in bad ones, they are bad.

In service marketing and selling, the logical reasons that you should win the business—your competence, your excellence, your talent—just pay the entry fees. Winning is a matter of feelings, and feelings are about personalities.

Meryl Streep is right. Life is like high school, and success in high school and service marketing often is largely a question of personality.

Be professional—but, more importantly, be personable.

PLANNING:
THE EIGHTEEN
FALLACIES

Fallacy: You Can Know What's Ahead

The three cornerstones of planning—predicting the future, seeing what you want your future to look like, and devising ways to make sure your future comes out that way—are shaky from the start.

Start with predicting the future. Don't. People can't. For example: Every significant business commentator in the 1950s insisted that the baby boom would create enormous unemployment when the boomers started entering the workforce in the 1960s. These experts goofed not once, but twice.

These experts failed to predict that women would flood the labor force. By the experts' reckoning, this flood should have created even more massive unemployment. Yet from 1965 to 1985, the labor force grew 40 percent, while the number of jobs grew 50 percent. That's more jobs, in both percentage and absolute numbers, than at any other time in America's peacetime history.

To see another bad prediction, look around your office. Dozens of experts predicted that huge numbers of your employees would be working from home. Surprise: Everyone's at work. The number of working-from-home employees is less than 30 percent of what most people predicted. (These experts failed to recognize that work performs a social function; most people *want* to be at an office.)

Weren't VCRs going to kill the movies? Movie attendance has surged since VCRs were introduced. It seems that only bad movies will kill the movies, and they're trying.

Wasn't television supposed to kill books? Well, books and mega-bookstores are proliferating. The reading group has become a social phenomenon. In fact, television probably has helped increase book sales. Would Norman Schwarzkopf's book have sold as many copies if the Gulf War had been covered only on radio? And does any technique sell more books than having the author appear on TV talk shows?

Speaking of bookstores: To appreciate why the future can't be predicted, go to your local bookstore. Go to the math section. Look at the top two rows. Chances are that those books discuss today's hot topic in mathematics: fractals. Fractals spring from chaos theory, which suggests the unpredictability and randomness of everything—even relationships among numbers.

If even numbers are unpredictable, and if you cannot predict something as physically based and data-rich as weather (where chaos theory first was postulated), then you certainly cannot predict people's attitudes.

Even if you can identify or predict people's attitudes, it's not that helpful, because behaviors don't always follow attitudes.

Take smoking: Given the almost universal awareness of smoking's risks since the first Surgeon

General's report, the virtual disappearance of stars smoking on television and in movies, and all the public condemnation and ridicule, smoking should be way down. It's not.

Take our eating habits: Health consciousness and the growing fear of cholesterol should have made the American steak house extinct. But six steak houses have opened in Minneapolis in the last four years, while not one has closed.

Sane, smart people—almost all planners are both—would have predicted just the opposite of these behaviors. Again, even if you can identify people's attitudes, you cannot predict the behavior that will follow.

So it seems that our efforts to plan are at the mercy of something that Einstein warned of, years ago:

"The universe is not only queerer than we suppose. It's queerer than we can suppose."

You never know. So don't assume that you should. Plan for several possible futures.

Fallacy: You Can Know What You Want

The second premise of planning—that you can know what you want in the future—is slightly dubious, too. George Bernard Shaw hit it squarely when he wrote, "There are two tragedies in life. One is not to get your heart's desire. The other is to get it."

Like almost everyone, I've always known what I wanted. Since 1962, it has been to be the next Arnold Palmer, the next editor of *Sports Illustrated*, the next F. Lee Bailey, the next David Ogilvy, and the next coach of the Minneapolis Cub 12 champions.

Businesses work the same way. They don't like what they once wanted, so they change their minds. Most want to get bigger, then realize that bigger often means less profitable. A few companies yearn to be the very best, then realize the market doesn't appreciate the quality and won't pay for it. Some companies want to attack a niche, then learn that their competitors had good reasons for avoiding that niche all those years.

The very premises on which planning is based seem flawed from the beginning.

Does this mean that you shouldn't plan? Not at all. It does mean that everyone involved in planning should start with three ideas:

First, accept the limitations of planning. Don't assume that putting eight smart people in a room with good data will automatically produce something. Ford put eight smart planners in a room, and out popped the Edsel.

Second, don't value planning for its result: the plan. The greatest value of the plan is the process, the thinking that went into it.

Third, don't plan your future. Plan your people. Outstanding people who fit your basic broad vision will tend to make the right decisions along the way, not by following a plan, but by using their skill.

Fallacy: Strategy Is King

Business once encouraged the view of strategy's superiority to tactics by throwing piles of money at it. Fifteen years ago, many with a Wharton MBA and a lust for money and status tried to get into strategic planning. They're still great jobs if you can get them. But after *Business Week* in 1984 reviewed the history of thirty-three major strategic plans, and found that nineteen had failed, the exalted status of strategic planners was in trouble.

Many business textbooks reinforce this bias about strategy's superiority. No surprise. Professors write textbooks, and most professors think that working on strategy sounds like a more dignified use of one's gifts than toiling on tactics.

But in successful companies, tactics drive strategy as much or more than strategy drives tactics. These companies do something and learn from it. It changes their thinking. As Tom Cooper, the former COO of Access Management, has observed, "Sometimes, the very first tactic you execute changes your entire plan."

For a vivid example of tactics shaping strategy, consider the Apple Macintosh computer. The Macintosh was not the first iteration of the Macintosh product; the Lisa was. Lisa bombed. But Lisa showed Apple what the market really needed. Guy Kawasaki, Macintosh's product manager, has admitted that Macintosh evolved from an explicit strategy:

Ready, fire, aim.

Or, as Kawasaki expresses it, "Lead, take a shot, listen, respond, lead again."

Tactics don't complete a process; they continue to shape one. Tactics sometimes are the end, the beginning, and the middle. Most important, tactics play a critical role—often the critical role—in information gathering. By contrast, you can't learn from your strategy. It's just sitting there pretending it knows what it's talking about, while your tactics are out there getting battle-tested by the market.

I once advised a consultant who was vacillating among several reasonable marketing tactics. I had a button printed with two words of advice for him:

Do Anything.

Fallacy: Build a Better Mousetrap

We still believe that if you build a better mousetrap, the world will start lining up on your porch. But too many examples today—computers and watches, to name two—suggest otherwise.

The computer industry has been packed with great ideas that were sitting in back rooms until someone dragged them out the door and pushed them with a passion. Xerox invented the mouse, icons, and windows. The ideas were great; but they were only ideas. Only Apple's passionate belief in those ideas put them into play—into the Macintosh computer—and changed the world.

This theme also played out with watches in the 1970s. The Swiss actually invented the quartz-powered digital watch, but held off introducing it. Then Hattori of Japan took the digital technology and started smashing the Swiss over the head with it, almost eliminating them from the watch market, with which "Swiss" had been synonymous for decades.

Consider the converse: If you execute your idea without passion, others will think you lack confidence in the idea, and they will lose confidence, too.

Execute passionately. Marginal tactics executed passionately almost always will outperform brilliant tactics executed marginally.

Fallacy: There'll Be a Perfect Time (The Bedrock Fallacy)

The too-typical planning effort can be illustrated by the fable of Bedrock Wheel Company.

Some Neanderthals were working on developing a wheel. Design toiled on different concepts—oblongs, rounded rectangles, and so forth—while Planning was considering some market applications.

Design finally created a prototype: a perfect circle. Sales and Marketing gushed. They knew they had a unique product with a huge market.

But Bedrock's Planners shouted, "Wait! Not so fast. We're not ready."

When pressed, the lead planner offered his visionary and ultimately disastrous reasons: "Look, you can see the trends. Men are tired of chasing woolly mammoths for food. So men will want to *ride* on these wheels. And men love speed; look, for example, at the way they have sex. So they'll want to go faster and faster on these wheels. That means you'll need wheels with traction—a smooth wheel won't work."

Naturally, an impatient fellow Bedrock executive finally asked, "So what do you recommend?"

"Simple," the prophetic planner announced.

"Delay the launch. We need to wait until man invents vulcanized rubber."

Preposterous? No; business. Years ago a Bloomington-based company created some astonishingly good multimedia software. This company wasn't just positioned to ride the multimedia wave—it *was* the wave. But the founders wanted an insanely great product. Did the world want that? No. The world wanted what the software company had right then. The world needed a plain old wheel and was ready to pay for it.

The company's endless analysis and waiting ended up proving that he who hesitates is lost. Other companies caught up and passed this company before the company released version 1.0.

Today's good idea almost always will beat tomorrow's better one.

Do it now. The business obituary pages are filled with planners who waited.

Fallacy: Patience Is a Virtue (The Shark Rule)

Most people believe that organizations work on the principle of inertia: Organizations tend to stay as they are, either at rest or in motion.

But it appears that organizations actually are subject to the law that governs sharks: If a shark does not move, it cannot breathe. And it dies.

Moving organizations tend to keep moving. Dormant ones tend to run out of air and die.

To worsen this problem, not moving rarely causes any immediate pain to an organization. This encourages even more waiting. "Hey, we waited to make sure we were right, and nothing bad happened, so that's good."

Not-moving begets more not-moving. By the time the delayed consequences of all this not-moving occur—one of which is that action-oriented people in the company flee the company, making the company even *more* waiting-oriented—it often is too late to correct them.

Act like a shark. Keep moving.

Fallacy: Think Smart (The Crab Concept)

At Carmichael-Lynch Advertising in the late 1980s, we conceived several awards for our group's creative people. My favorite was the Crab Plaque.

This plaque, awarded for the Stupidest Idea, featured a windup plastic crab, because crabs move laterally, symbolizing the power of lateral thinking. Because lateral ideas do not follow in a straight line from the thinking that preceded them, they usually look stupid at first.

But we needed more stupid thinking. We had too much smart thinking; our average Stanford-Binet exceeded 120, easy. We just needed to be stupider—and to be unafraid of coming up with seemingly stupid ideas, which often turn out the best.

As we learned every day, highly intelligent people are the world's foremost experts at squashing good ideas. That's because intelligent people have one absolute favorite use for their formidable intelligence: telling other people, with total conviction and logic, why other people's ideas will not work.

Planning tends to attract these people, but they are dangerous. As smart as they are, their memories fail them; they always forget that good ideas often sound ludicrous at first.

Think dumb.

The Fallacy of Science and Data

Nothing said in a business meeting can match the force of any statement preceded by the words "The research shows . . ."

That's because "research" connotes something scientific. But there are no rigorous sciences of human behavior. The social sciences consist, at best, of some well-supported general observations.

Planning research is not research in the best scientific sense. It's insurance. The former research director of a large food company, in fact, confessed that he actually called his department the Insurance Department. Product managers would ask him for scientific support for their plans so they could go face top management after their product bombed and say, "Well, hey, the Research said it would work."

Many people still give special weight to any statement that is highly quantified, as if they believe that numbers have scientific weight. "Most people prefer New Coke to Old Coke" sounds suspect to them. "Five out of six people" sounds much better. But "83.3 percent of respondents" sounds like convincing scientific data. Never mind that the last two statements—"Five out of six" and "83.3 percent"—actually are identical. And never mind that all three statements turned out to be totally inaccurate and misleading, as executives at Coca-Cola learned to their public embarrassment.

This aura of science has a remarkable ability to fool people. Consider Stanford Research Institute's introduction of the VALs (Values, Attitudes, and Lifestyles) concept to marketing planning in the mid-1980s. VALs concluded that there are seven types of people, a conclusion that many people initially bought. Did those people forget who they were?

Like everyone else, these people had met thousands of people and from that, learned that each person is unique. These people had searched for friendships and found very few people with whom they shared even a few things in common. But when the VALs people came along—well-educated people linked to a great university—and said, "There are seven types of people," many bought it.

Before long, commercials were touting coffee as the drink for "the New Achievers" (the largest-VALs segment during that Yuppie era)—the comic highlight of the mercifully brief VALs boom.

Today, even "hard" scientists confess that their sciences look softer every day. And the "soft" sciences have little claim to science at all, even when they offer broad generalizations backed by numbers.

My friend John Tillman, a brilliant student of the hard sciences, once explained why he never studied one prominent social science. "Sociology," John insisted, "consists of systematic and fancy ways of describing what already is obvious."

Mistrust "facts." And don't approach planning as a precise science. Planning is an imprecise art.

The Fallacy of Focus Groups

Occasionally, one plus one equals more than two.

Bill Bernbach discovered that in the late 1950s, when he brought new imagination to advertising by bringing a new method to it.

The method was the copywriter and art director team. Before Bernbach, most copywriters and art directors worked independently. The copywriter came up with an idea, a headline, and some copy for an ad, and slipped his notes under the art director's door. The art director dressed up the idea, made a layout, and voilà! an ad.

Bernbach believed in brainstorming, the process in which ideas ricochet between at least two people. He believed that if individuals can produce good ideas, teams can produce even better ones.

Then Bernbach's teams at Doyle Dane Bernbach created the ads for Avis, Volkswagen, and Polaroid that proved Bernbach right.

Given that groups are good at brainstorming, perhaps many services might benefit from focus groups that brainstorm new ideas.

They might. But consider the major innovations in service marketing: automated teller machines, negotiable certificates of deposit, storefront tax services, legal clinics, predictive dialing systems, traveler's checks, overnight package delivery, automated airline reservations systems, junk bonds, frequent flyer and other loyalty marketing programs, credit cards, money market mutual funds, extended service contracts, home equity lines of credit, alternative dispute resolution services, drive-in and drive-up services, home delivery, database marketing, home shopping, and a dozen others.

Did focus groups generate *any* of those ideas?

Could a focus group have generated any of those ideas?

Could a focus group inspire the personal computer, personal copier, cellular telephone, electronic digital assistant, fax machine—or anything like them?

And while we are on this subject, consider three recent innovations: skinless Kentucky Fried Chicken, McLean (lower-calorie McDonald's hamburgers), and low-fat Pizza Hut pizzas. Focus groups *loved* these ideas. Real people, unfortunately, did not, and KFC, McDonald's, and Pizza Hut abandoned all three products.

So maybe focus groups can brainstorm for you.

But you should never bet on it.

Beware of focus groups; they focus only on today. And planning is about tomorrow.

The Fallacy of Memory

The gifted science writer Stephen Jay Gould once wrote a wonderful essay on how our memories deceive us. For years, Gould remembered the sunny afternoons of his youth, talking with his dad on the steps leading into the Forest Hills Tennis Center.

Several years ago, Gould was walking in his old neighborhood. Suddenly he saw those steps.

They led up to the dilapidated door of Mueller Moving and Storage.

We remember badly. We look back and see things that were not there. We cite as proof for something an event that simply did not occur as we remember it.

In planning, beware of what you think you remember.

The Fallacy of Experience

They say people learn from experience. Some do.

But consider what one Minnesota company thought it learned from its advertising. In 1988 the company used some fairly obscure Minnesota celebrities as spokespersons in some unremarkable national television ads. The ads flopped. The marketing director, of course, confidently concluded that using celebrities in ads doesn't work.

The people at Nike should speak with her.

In the early 1980s, a Minnesota dairy ran an internationally acclaimed radio campaign featuring the dairy's foreman. One spring morning, a dairy executive received an angry letter. The elderly woman author was upset over a commercial in which Ord Paulsen, the foreman, said that the dairy's prize cow reminded him of his wife. Meeting with two agency people afterward, the executive read the letter, hurled it into his desk, and insisted that the agency kill the campaign. The letter confirmed, in the executive's exact words, that "these spots use humor. *And people do not like humor.*"

When we infer things, we tend to overgeneralize. We want to establish cubbyholes and some general principles. And so we decide that celebrities never work in ads, that people do not like humor—and a dozen other examples of concluding too much from too little.

What does what you experience really prove? Usually, far less than you thought. And what you thought you learned can make you abandon a strategy or tactic that was 90 percent right.

Have a healthy distrust of what experience has taught you.

The Fallacy of Confidence

You know several things about your business:

"Our customers buy on price.

"Telemarketing does not work with this audience.

"Our clients won't pay for higher quality, even if we could achieve it."

You know things like these. Or do you?

You hear similar sacred truths in every company.

Often, these sacred truths start with someone—we'll call him Will—as a mere opinion. Will then starts seeing everything in light of his opinion. He leaps on any evidence that supports his opinion and ignores all contrary evidence. Before long, Will's opinion has become his conviction, which he conveys to other employees. Will's apostles, impressed by his reputation and conviction, spread Will's faith further. Soon, Will's mere opinion has become a company-wide dogma.

But many of these so-called truths are false. Just like many of *your* truths about *your* service.

This sobering fact—that you, Will, and I are wrong *far* more often than we know—has been suggested by dozens of studies that test people on subjects on which they consider themselves authorities. The people tested answer a series of questions, and then answer this question about each answer: "From one to a hundred percent, how certain are you about this answer?"

What happens?

On the answers of which people say they are totally—100 percent—certain, they are right only 85 percent of the time.

In other words, 15 percent of the time you think you are absolutely certain you are absolutely wrong.

In most services, that 15 percent error—those wrong but widespread assumptions that everyone in the company is making—is the most leverageable part of your business. *Find it, and attack it.*

If you are prone to being certain, copy Jay Chiat. The head of Chiat Day, the ad agency behind many of America's most conspicuous advertisements, Chiat carries a note in his pocket. The note reminds him that whenever he is in an argument he should remember the note's three words:

Maybe he's right.

Maybe others *are* right and you're wrong—even if you are certain you're right. These tests, which demonstrate the fallacy of confidence ("the overconfidence bias," as it is called by psychologists), also tell you not to be overwhelmed by *other* people's total convictions. In fact, many businesses unwittingly follow the Path of Greatest Conviction; they consistently do whatever the most convinced person argues they should do.

So those Question Authority bumper stickers offer good advice. Even when you or someone else feels certain, you *should* question that authority.

Especially your own.

Beware of the overconfidence bias. Maybe he's right.

Fallacy: Perfection Is Perfection

You easily can get stalled in the shift from strategy to tactics because you are paralyzed by your desire for excellence.

Here's a good way to rank The Best Plans:

a) Very good
b) Good
c) Best
d) Not good
e) Truly god-awful

Best ranks lower than good? Why?
Because getting to best usually gets complicated.
First, can everyone ever agree on what is best?
How long will it take to reach an agreement?
How long will it take to achieve best?

How much excellence in other areas—work environment, productivity, speed of delivery—will we sacrifice to achieve excellence in this one?

And perhaps most important, will all that excellence really benefit the person for whom it is intended? Will the prospects or customers care? Will it be worth the cost to them?

The planning process tends to attracts perfectionists. But something paralyzes these people: their fear that executing the plan will show that the plan was *not* perfect. So rather than risk being found out, these people do nothing. They wait.

Many outstanding big-picture thinkers are always looking for, and burdened by, this search for perfection. But too often, the path to perfection leads to procrastination.

Don't let perfect ruin good.

Fallacy: Failure Is Failure

Few phobias are more widespread than the fear of failure.

But what is failure?

Robert Townsend, who helped mastermind Avis's dramatic turnaround in the 1960s, said two of every three decisions he made were wrong.

America's best pro basketball teams lose the basketball every three minutes without even getting up a shot.

The legendary golfer Ben Hogan said that in eighteen holes, he usually hit only two or three balls exactly as he had planned.

Fred Smith got a C on the graduate business school paper in which he described the concept for Federal Express.

The world champion in baseball has to win only 57 percent of its championship games.

And no discussion of failure should avoid 3M. 3M went almost two years without a sale. Then in 1904 they tried sandpaper. Two years later sandpaper sales were averaging $2,500 a month—on expenses of over $9,000 a month. William McKnight became the assistant bookkeeper in 1907, settled for stock instead of cash while the company bounced from blunder to blunder, and retired with over $500 million in 1978.

There's little point in killing an idea by saying it might fail. *Any* idea might fail. If you're doing anything worthwhile at all, you'll suffer a dozen failures.

Start failing so you can start succeeding.

The Fallacy of Expertise

Before you look to expert insight for help in planning, ask yourself: What is an expert?

The *Wall Street Journal* periodically matches the nation's leading stock analysts against a handful of darts. Over the past year, the randomly thrown darts consistently have hit better stocks on a dartboard than those chosen by the experts, after months of study and years of experience.

What is an expert? Is an expert anything more than someone with lots of data and experience? But to what end? The data on most subjects will support totally opposite conclusions—a fact which explains the popularity of *The McLaughlin Group* and similar televised debates.

The value of an "expert"'s experience is dubious for another reason. Every experience in life is unique. Anytime that we apply the apparent lessons of one experience to another one, we tend to assume that the two experiences are essentially identical.

They *never* are.

Don't look to experts for all your answers. There are no answers, only informed opinions.

The Fallacy of Authority

Chances are, your organization runs on the Alpha Principle. Ideas do not follow the good thinking in an organization; ideas follow the power.

Most organizations work like the groups of apes from which we evolved. The alphas dictate what the group does and thinks.

But are alphas better at decision making? Not necessarily. Alphas are just better at getting and keeping power. In most organizations, in fact, alphas are the people who just look and sound like they *should* have the power (a conclusion suggested by several studies that show that height, not business school performance, is the strongest predictor of an MBA's starting salary).

If your smart people don't kill your ideas, chances are the alphas will.

If you're an alpha, learn to shut up. Imitate Ben Taylor, the alpha who runs the Executrain franchise in Minnesota, often the most successful of America's very successful Executrain franchises. When asked to explain his success, Taylor's first response is "I listen."

The bumper stickers are right: Question Authority. Question alphas.

The Fallacy of Common Sense

A client once told me that "doing a marketing plan is simple. It's just common sense."

Unfortunately, common sense is not that common.* What seems common, in fact, is people acting contrary to their own experience—recall again those people who accepted VALs in the 1980s. Or worse, people act against their obvious self-interest—a human habit that inspired an entire book, *The March of Folly*, by historian Barbara Tuchman. As famous examples, Tuchman cites Montezuma surrendering to an Aztec army the size of your high school PE class, and the Trojans deciding, "Hey, the Greeks left this huge horse behind. Let's haul it back into our city."

My client's faith in common sense was misplaced for another reason. He was right in thinking that most people possess enough common sense to draw a logical conclusion from a premise. But in planning, people do not stumble in reaching conclusions. They err in establishing their premises.

Take Burger King's stumble, for example.

---

*Common sense, as one example, argues that you advertise automobiles by appealing to potential car buyers. As proof of the folly of that kind of common sense, and evidence that car advertising must appeal to dealers, see *When the Suckers Moon*, Randal Rothenberg's engaging book on Wieden & Kennedy's ill-fated "What to Drive" campaign for Subaru.

For years, Burger King operated from these premises: "(a) People come to us for food, and (b) Most people prefer the taste of flame-broiled burgers." From those premises, Burger King executives reached this commonsense conclusion: "Therefore, we should stress our flame-broiled burgers as the reason to switch to us."

Irrefutable logic—but premise (a) was all wrong. People do not go to fast-food restaurants to satisfy a desire for something delicious. They go for something fast, cheap, and palatable that satisfies their hunger. Burger King displayed good common sense, but it cost them millions—because their premise was all wrong.

Whenever it does show up, common sense helps in any discipline. (My surgeon father said that 90 percent of orthopedic surgery is common sense. Woody Allen hinted at the same thing when he said that 90 percent of success is showing up.) Basically, marketing planning involves a finite number of broad strategies—create genuine distinction, lead on price, seize an untapped niche and migrate, and some others—from which some common sense will certainly help you choose. The hard and critical part comes next.

How do you execute that strategy? How do you fill a niche's needs? How do you create uniqueness? How do you interest and convert prospects? Better yet, how do you interest and convert your own people?

How do you succeed?

In this realm, the realm of tactics, your options are infinite. This makes common sense virtually irrelevant. At this stage, common sense is a shield rather than a sword. It can protect you, but it cannot fight the battle.

Common sense did not inspire the great marketing innovations of this century—the L.L. Bean boot, personal computer, overnight delivery, or any other. Leaps of imagination created them.

Common sense will only get you so far. For inspiring results, you'll need inspiration.

The Fallacy of Fate

Speaking to the strategic planning committee for Temple Israel in Minneapolis, I began a discussion of this fallacy with a quote from the movie *My Favorite Year:* "Jews always know two things. Suffering, and where to find great Chinese food."

I also told them that it was no surprise that *The Power of Positive Thinking* was written by a white Protestant. I asked them, "Hey, can you imagine somebody named Goldberg writing a book on positive thinking?"

While I already knew that Jewish jokes play well to Jewish audiences, my motive was quite serious. There are fatalistic groups, fatalistic people, and fatalistic companies. Some people cannot picture success. Some people are afraid to believe in it because they are terrified of disappointment. And most people will say, "We tried something like that. Didn't work."

The New York Mets didn't have a prayer in the 1969 World Series. They had been laughed at for years. Their relief pitcher Tug McGraw implored them, "Ya gotta believe." They started believing.

Their opponents, the Baltimore Orioles, wish they hadn't.

You gotta believe.

ANCHORS, WARTS, AND AMERICAN EXPRESS: HOW PROSPECTS THINK

Yeah, but I Like It

Here's a good question: Why *do* people buy what they buy?

Many service marketers assume that buying decisions are fairly logical. A prospect for a service adds up the cost and benefits of one service, compares it to another's, and chooses the service with the better score.

Providers of many services—accountants, lawyers, and financial services particularly—are prone to this notion that people really are *homo sapiens*—wise primates—who make wise, rational decisions based on objective analyses of costs and benefits.

But seemingly sophisticated prospects for even sophisticated services do not behave this way, as the strange case of Visa vs. American Express clearly suggests.

As the judge for this case, consider the evidence.

Visa cards are accepted in almost three times more locations than American Express cards.

You can pay back a Visa card immediately or over time. You must pay on an American Express card at the end of each month or suffer substantial penalties and testy little notices from Chicago.

You pay $20 for a basic Visa card, and $55 for one from American Express.

Now, what truly rational people want from a credit card is *utility relative to price*. If they are being logical, they want to be able to use the card wherever and whenever they buy and have the option to pay their balance immediately to save interest charges or over time, if necessary. Truly rational people also want to pay as little as possible for those benefits.

A truly rational person, in other words, chooses a Visa card. Perhaps all of Earth's rational people do choose Visa cards. But that leaves approximately 25 million Americans who use American Express cards. Why?

Because of prestige, apparently. That is, American Express emphasizes that "membership has its privileges," and that privilege of membership in American Express is in being part of an "elite" club, an enormous "elite"—25 million people—by the way.

Logical?

Now, some people might argue that their services are different and that their prospects are more rational than credit card buyers. But, dear service executives, those American Express cardholders are prospects for *your* service, too. And few prospects for most services can intelligently evaluate the rational features of your and other services and make an informed, rational choice.

Your prospects feel like the jurors in case after case. Befuddled by the facts and often mistrustful of the parties offering those facts, these jurors look beyond the facts, to things like the shine of the defendant's shoes, the niceness of the defendant's attorney, and a dozen other irrelevant details.

Appeal only to a prospect's reason, and you may have no appeal at all.

How Prospects Decide: Choosing the Familiar

In 1988, two telemarketing companies began business.

In Omaha, Nebraska, Steve Edleman established Edleman Telemarketing with a hundred stations, some contacts, and a full-page ad on the back of *Telemarketing* magazine. The ad was a huge investment for such a small company, an investment that Edleman has continued to make every month for what is now seven years.

Three months later, in Minneapolis, Gary Cohen and Rick Diamond opened ACI Telemarketing with superior technology and a strong pitch.

Today, Edleman Telemarketing is the giant of the industry. ACI is just as competent, but much smaller.

Edleman's success suggests how prospects make decisions. They rely on familiarity. From ad after full-page ad, prospects had heard more about Edleman. So whenever they were in doubt—which was often—prospects chose Edleman.

People choose what seems most familiar. It's the same bias that makes people think that more people die from motor vehicle accidents than from stomach cancer. We tend to choose the one we hear the most about—even though the truth is that stomach cancer kills twice as many people as car accidents.

Another small surprise: The evidence suggests

that it is better to be known badly than not to be known at all. This is due to a human trait called attribute forgetting. Let's say you hear something negative about a company. As time passes you tend to forget that negative information—you forget the attributes—and remember only the company name. Then, asked which company you have a better opinion of—that first company or another company you have never heard of—you choose the familiar company, even though everything you heard about that company was negative. Familiarity wields that much power.

You need to make yourself familiar to your prospects. You need to get out there.

Familiarity breeds business. Spread your word however you can.

How Prospects Decide: Using the Most Recent Data

Now, what do you do against a competitor who is more familiar to your prospect than you are—someone who simply is taking up more space in your prospect's brain?

You try to take advantage of another bias of people: the Recency Effect.

The IRS understands this principle very well, too.

Every March, the IRS plants in papers across the country the story of a huge tax evasion prosecution. (In his valuable book *Influence*, Robert Cialdini points out that the IRS-planted stories have become so common that the *Chicago Tribune* headlined its 1982 story "Annual Tax Warning: Twenty Indicted Here.") That recent information makes it easier for people to decide not to take phony deductions.

Companies that often present competitive pitches know how the Recency Effect works. These companies—at least the smarter ones—do everything possible to be the last company to present. It's the home field advantage in many service industries.

There are several ways to take advantage of the Recency Effect; they could fill a chapter by themselves.

The essential point is that you should *always* take advantage of this effect, with a follow-up that is as well conceived and powerful as anything in your presentation.

This is not the time to sound predictable and only slightly enthusiastic.

Do that, and a shrewd competitor will say something stronger and more effective—and grab the business.

Take advantage of the Recency Effect. Follow up brilliantly.

How Prospects Decide: Choosing "Good Enough"

Two years ago, I lost in a presentation for a client for whom I was clearly the superior choice. No one within two time zones knew as much as I did about the client's industry. No one had more success generating business in that industry. My competitors had no business pitching the account.

That's just what I thought. And unfortunately, that's just what I communicated.

I lost, of course. That loss reminded me of a basic fact in human decision making. People do not look to make the superior choice; they want to avoid making a bad choice.

Experts on decision making call this Looking for Good Enough. It happens day after day, in decision after decision. It happened, in fact, the day I wrote this section.

The Minneapolis *Star Tribune* featured that event in a headline: "Breyer Was Third Choice." Bill Clinton had to fill a vacancy on the Supreme Court left by the retirement of Harry Blackmun. Clinton wanted Bruce Babbitt, his Secretary of Interior. But that would have created a cabinet vacancy and might have produced an embarrassing confirmation fight. Babbitt was risky.

Clinton also liked appellate judge Richard Arnold. But Arnold had health problems and a record that might have aroused opposition from women.

So Clinton chose Stephen Breyer, despite Breyer's limited judicial experience. As Clinton's Special Counsel Lloyd Cutler told the press, "Breyer had the fewest problems."

Clinton, like millions of other people every day, did not choose the most qualified candidate, the jurist with the best chance of achieving greatness. Clinton looked for "good enough," and chose the man with the fewest minuses.

Looking for Good Enough happens repeatedly in business, too. So whenever you make your pitch, ask yourself, "What risks might a prospect see in hiring us?" Then, without reminding the prospects of those risks—which will only remind your prospects of their fears—eliminate the prospect's fears, one by one.

In my case, I needed to eliminate two fears. Because I was an expert, they feared I would be prohibitively expensive and uncompromising. And because I had worked for larger clients on larger projects, they feared I would not consider their project important.

But I never addressed those fears. I got so carried away telling them I was a superior choice that I forgot to assure them I would be a good choice.

Forget looking like the superior choice. Make yourself an excellent choice.

Then eliminate <u>anything</u> that might make you a bad choice.

The Anchoring Principle

Joan Davis, unwittingly, enters Smithers & Company as a secretary.

For months she tries to convince her boss that she belongs in management. Joan's boss finally relents and persuades his boss to give Joan a try. She tries. Unfortunately, a widespread belief soon takes hold that Joan "is not quite right for the job." Discouraged, she leaves for Apogee & Company. Four years later, Joan is named Apogee's vice president.

After spinning a wheel that stops on the number 800, a researcher asks a group how many words Lincoln used in the Gettysburg Address. The group's average answer is eight hundred. After spinning a wheel that stops on the number 275, the researcher asks the same question of a second group. Their average answer is two hundred seventy-five.

Peter goes to an office for an interview. Sarah, his interviewer, does what several studies of interviewing predict that she will do: She makes her decision after Peter has spoken for less than one minute.

What do these cases have in common? The Anchoring Principle. The people in Smithers & Company were anchored to their initial perception of Joan as a "mere secretary." The subjects in the Gettysburg Address test (a test similar to many tests that demonstrate this principle) were anchored to those numbers they saw on the wheel, even though the numbers have no relationship to the Gettysburg Address. Job interviewer Sarah was anchored to Peter's first appearance and first words.

As these examples show, people do not simply form impressions. They get *anchored* to them.

Even more important, people with little time—almost all people today—are more apt to make first impressions as snap judgments, and then base all their later decisions on them. The smart marketer must be aware of this strong tendency. First impressions have never been more critical—they take hold very quickly, and they become the anchors to which you and your success are tied.

What anchors have the prospect already attached to you?

How can you overcome them?

What first impression do you make? What's the first thing you say? The first way that you position your service?

Identify and polish your anchors.

Last Impressions Last

Charlie Brown notices that the fronts of Linus's shoes are freshly shined, but the backs are scuffed. He points this out to Linus. Linus tells Charlie he knows; he meant to shine them that way.

"I care about what people think of me when I

enter a room," Linus says. "I don't care what they think when I leave."

Linus has made one of his rare mistakes.

In repeated studies, people shown a sequence of items—pictures of an apple, pear, peach, prune, and pomegranate, for example—are most apt to remember the apple and the pomegranate. They remember the first and the last items but forget the middle.

Recognizing this special power of first and last impressions, advertisers willingly pay premium prices for ads in the very front and very back of magazines.

Teachers of writing also recognize this principle when they encourage writers to put their strongest points at the start and finish of each sentence and paragraph, and the filler in the middle.

The people who manage KinderCare facilities, a national franchise of child care centers, recognize this Rule of Last Impressions, too. "If a child ends the day on a happy note," John Kaegi, KinderCare senior vice president for marketing, once observed, "that's going to carry over into the next morning and the next day."

The rule of last impressions is reflected in dozens of ways. Consider apologies and forgiveness, for example. The last impression a person makes, by apologizing, often obscures the person's memory of the event that led to the apology.

Each impression you make will—temporarily, at least—be your last. So make it strong.

Risky Business

Joel and Judy Wethall are driving from Tampa to Disney World when they are struck with hunger. They begin watching for places to eat, then choose a Burger King restaurant.

Their choice seems odd; they dislike Whopper hamburgers. Why *did* they choose Burger King?

Their alternatives were two unknowns: two local restaurants with nice facades and hints of quality. Had they tried either restaurant, they would have enjoyed juicier hamburgers, fresher salads, and friendly personal service, right to their table.

What were the Wethalls thinking? What almost every prospect for every service thinks. They were not looking for the service they wanted most but the one they feared the least. They did not choose a good experience; they chose to minimize the risk of a bad experience.

This intelligent couple was duplicating what happened all over the country that day, among people choosing accounting firms, remodelers, dry cleaners, cleaning services, human resources consultants, and thousands of other services. They were not expressing their preference. They were *minimizing their risk.*

Yes, build the quality into your service—but make it less risky, too.

You Have Nothing to Fear but Your Client's Fear Itself

Peggy, your prospect, is frightened.

You are just this invisible thing—a service—a mere promise that you will do something.

Peggy is afraid. She is thinking about buying something almost sight unseen.

She is very uneasy—and she is the typical prospect.

Often, Peggy is so fearful she does not buy, even though she needs and could benefit from your service, and even though you are the best company she could choose.

It is less risky for Peggy to do nothing.

At this point, you do not need to put more sale in. You need to take some of the fear out.

How?

How do product manufacturers do it? They offer free home trials, or free money-back guarantees.

Can you do that? Often, you can. Instead of asking for the business, ask for a project. Offer to do one shirt, one small survey, one blurb for a newsletter, one small case, one free review of their retirement plan. If it is a big account, ask for a tiny slice—a slice about which Peggy might not worry and on which you can shine.

Always remember: Peggy is *afraid*.

The best thing you can do for a prospect is eliminate her fear. Offer a trial period or a test project.

Show Your Warts

In the mid-1980s, some researchers at Cleveland State University made a startling discovery.

The researchers created for two fictitious job candidates—Dave and John—two identical résumés, and two almost identical letters of reference. The only difference was that John's letter included the sentence "Sometimes, John can be difficult to get along with."

The researchers showed the résumés to personnel directors. Which candidate did the directors most want to interview?

Sometimes-Difficult-to-Get-Along-With John.

The researchers concluded that the criticism of John made the reference's praise of John seem more believable, and that made John look like a stronger candidate. Showing John's warts actually helped sell John.

But does this academic study apply in the real world? Ask Tom Keacher. A regional sales manager for First Protection, the company that originated marine service contracts, Tom for years started his sales presentations by listing every boat engine part that First Protection covered. Midway through 1994, however, Tom decided to switch tactics. He started his pitches by listing every part that the service contract did not cover. The result? Tom's conversion rate improved significantly.

Rather than hide your weaknesses, admit them.

That will make you look honest and trustworthy—a key to selling a service.

Tell the truth. Even if it hurts, it will help.

Business Is in the Details

People who insist, "The companies in our industry are basically alike" must recognize a human trait.

People feel a need to justify their decisions to themselves. So they look for *differences* upon which to base their decision.

What does this mean to a company in an industry of lookalikes?

It means that the more alike two services are, the more important each difference becomes.

With meaningful differences difficult to find, prospects look for signals in seemingly trivial differences: the decor of the lobby, the color of the business card, the heft of the brochure, even the smell of the salesperson's cologne. Unable to see the real differences between the services, prospects look for clues to differences elsewhere.

It bears repeating:

The more similar the services, the more important the differences.

In fact, much of effective service management can be described as the careful management of the seemingly inconsequential.

Accentuate the trivial.

THE MORE YOU SAY,
THE LESS PEOPLE HEAR:
POSITIONING AND FOCUS

Fanatical Focus

Ask the pizza man. Successful marketing starts with positioning.

This principle is the focus of Al Ries and Jack Trout's marketing classic, *Positioning*. In its most important essentials, *Positioning* says:

1. You must position yourself in your prospect's mind.
2. Your position should be singular: one simple message.
3. Your position must set you apart from your competitors.
4. You must sacrifice. You cannot be all things to all people; you must focus on one thing.

Domino's vividly illustrates strong service positioning. For years, Domino's never mentioned quality, price, or value. Instead, Domino's relentlessly stressed its speed: "30 Minutes or It's On Us," ad after ad after ad.

As a result, Domino's came to "own" the distinctive concept of speed in the pizza delivery business. When people thought of fast, reliable delivery, they thought of Domino's.

Today, when reporters ask Domino's president, Tom Monaghan, the secret of his success, what does he answer?

"A fanatical *focus* on doing *one* thing well."

Stand for one distinctive thing that will give you a competitive advantage.

The Fear of Positioning

A quick quiz:

Which terrifies service marketers most:

A) The suggestion that they must position their service?

B) The shower scene in *Psycho*?

The correct answer is A.

Why all the fear? Because standing for one thing means you cannot expressly stand for other things. You must *sacrifice*.

"NO! We cannot give up that business! We have to say we are this and this and this! We're sacrificing opportunity. Forget it!"

Rather than sacrificing opportunities, a narrow focus often creates opportunities. For vivid proof, consider Scandinavian Airlines. In 1980, faced with $20 million in losses, SAS executives decided to position the airline as "the business traveler's airline." Listen carefully and you almost can hear, all the way from Stockholm, the hollering that preceded that decision:

"What, and sacrifice tourist travelers? Run ads with blond Yuppies in Power Suits? The tourists will ditch us! We *have* to address them."

The sacrificers, however, won their argument for the business traveler's position. And they won something else: *more tourist customers*.

It worked like this:

SAS created EuroClass for business travelers. EuroClass had olives in the martinis, bigger seats, phones, telexes, a separate four-minute-faster check-in counter, and free drinks, newspapers, and magazines.

The move revived SAS: The airline made $80 million profit in EuroClass's first year. But something else happened. Because business travelers fly at full fares, airlines earn much bigger margins on business travelers. By filling up so many seats with full-fare passengers, SAS could afford to dump prices on the remaining seats. That is, they could offer even lower fares to tourists.

And they did. Soon, SAS was blessed with the highest percentage of full-fare travelers of any European airline—and the lowest tourist fares in all of Europe, too.

In short, positioning SAS as the most desirable airline for business travelers made it the most desirable airline to business travelers *and* tourists.

Some sacrifice.

To broaden your appeal, narrow your position.

Lesser Logic

Around the time that SAS began its dramatic revival, a New York City law firm was plotting a similar success. While somewhat inadvertent—as the firm's partners now admit—the dramatic ascent of Skadden, Arps, Slate, Meagher & Flom is yet another example of the power of focus.

First, some background. The best-regarded New York City law firms have long been dominated by WASP gentlemen from Harvard and Yale and the "right" clubs. A gentleman lawyer truly is a gentle man. Except to defend his country from naked aggression or his wife from naked slander, a gentleman does not fight.

That ethic meant that gentlemen lawyers did not engage in the bloodiest fights in business: takeovers. So when mergers and acquisitions came into prominence in the 1970s, New York's gentlemanly law firms regarded M&A the way other natives of India regard the Untouchables. This aversion in turn created an opportunity in the New York legal market into which Joe Flom happily jumped.

The driving force and chief rainmaker for Skadden Arps, Flom had few choices. Flom, like most of his partners, went to the wrong school (City College of New York) and belonged to none of the right clubs. For Flom to position Skadden Arps as an M&A specialist did not require courage; it required only an appetite and a mortgage, two things that Flom and each of his partners had.

But Skadden's specialization—its narrow focus on M&A—soon had its dramatic effect. From dominating the M&A work of the seventies and eighties, Skadden Arps soon spread into every area of old-line work. By 1989, the firm had gross revenues of $517.5

million—enough to qualify for the *Fortune* 500 and by far the world's richest law firm.

That greatest success all started with Flom's narrow focus. Focusing on M&A made Skadden very appealing to clients for a simple reason. However ugly takeovers may be, a lawyer's ability to handle them clearly demonstrates the skill to handle complex cases and people, and to stay graceful under pressure. In short, if you can do M&As, you can do almost anything.

Skadden's success illustrates the lesser logic power of some positions. Skadden's position in a narrow but complex area appealed to clients with less complex problems. "If they can do something that hard, *then by lesser logic* they can do this."

Ask yourself: What special skill could your business develop and communicate that would, by lesser logic, position you strongly in other areas? What is the big skill you could develop and market that clearly implies other valuable skills?

In your service, what's the hardest task? Position yourself as the expert at this task, and you'll have lesser logic in your corner.

Halo Effects

Why do people in services fear positioning so much? Because they fear that standing for one thing will limit their appeal. But it doesn't work that way, for one important reason: People *associate*.

We tend to think, for example, that attractive people are smarter, friendlier, more honest, and more reliable than less attractive people. We associate one positive thing—attractiveness—with many other good things.

We assume that poor people lack initiative and intelligence, are less trustworthy, and are less concerned with cleanliness and appearance, when few if any of these characteristics are displayed by one poor person we may see. We associate; we automatically link one negative thing—poverty—with many other negative things.

It's how people are programmed. It's how your prospects think.

The interesting case of Long Island Bank and Trust, cited in *Positioning*, demonstrates the Halo Effect in marketing a service.

Bank personnel tested people's perceptions of the bank, then ran several ads stressing that Long Island was *the* local bank for Long Island. The ads did not mention assets, range of services, or quality of services. After running the ads, the bank tested people's perceptions of the bank again—and discovered something remarkable.

People now had stronger perceptions of *every-thing* about the bank: its number of branches, range of services, quality of services, and capital.

So the next time you say, "But we have to say this, and this, and this, and this; it's all important," remember Long Island Bank and Trust—and the power of the Halo Effect.

*Say one positive thing, and you will become **associated** with many.*

No Two Services Are the Same

In a positioning exercise, if you ask a principal of a service company, "What makes your service different?" you often get a disappointing response.

"Honestly, nothing. We're all pretty much the same."

He's wrong. Every service is different, and creating and communicating differences is central to effective marketing.

History shows that *everything* can be made different. For years, catsups, flour, pickles, and sugar—to name only four products—came in large tubs and were sold as commodities in corner stores. Then Heinz, Gold Medal, and C&H came along, turned these apparently indistinguishable commodities into distinctive brands, and made billions.

If buyers can perceive differences in different cat-sups, flour, pickles, and sugar—all of which are almost identical biologically and chemically—then people certainly will perceive major differences in services. Services, after all, comprise unique compo-nents: people, no two of whom are the same.

Two services cannot be virtually identical in the people they attract, the work they inspire, the infor-mation and training they pass on, the rate at which they learn, or the efficiency with which they work. It is not unlikely; it is *impossible.* Human beings are too different, and their interactions in different envi-ronments only magnify those differences.

What's more, prospects perceive services as dif-ferent. All of us have walked into a company and immediately detected the forces at work. Passion, energy, optimism—in a dynamic service company, all these qualities are palpable within the first fifteen seconds of entering the lobby. You can read the DNA of a company from the receptionist and dis-cover it replicated throughout the company.

Every service is different. Identifying and commu-nicating those differences and creating new ones are central to successful service marketing.

If you cannot see the differences in your service, look harder.

Position Is a Passive Noun, Not an Active Verb

We want to position ourselves as the market leader," say several million executives each year.

They cannot do that.

They cannot position themselves as the leader for a simple reason:

No company can position itself as anything.

You can focus your efforts and your message, which sometimes can influence your position. But your position is a place, and someone else puts you there: your prospects.

Even services that do nothing to market their company have a position. A prospect simply takes what he knows about the company and positions the company accordingly.

Take the position of my native state of Oregon, the last stop on the train to heaven. For years, the state has tried to attract more tourists. Among the obstacles the state confronts—including the fact that many people know nothing about Oregon—is the state's position in the minds of many other people: that place where it always rains.

Unless the state of Oregon spends $15 million a year on television advertising for the next fifteen years, that is the position it will occupy: the Rainy State.

Given that, perhaps the most effective thing that Oregon could do to attract tourism would be to begin with that Rain State position, and make it a benefit. To wit, run ads showing a thundering rainstorm over Mount Hood, with the voice-over solemnly announcing, "From Thanksgiving to Memorial Day every year [crackling thunder], Oregonians endure all of this [pounding rain] . . ."

The screen then shifts to the view of a spectacular green forest, Portland's gorgeous Rose Garden, Oregon's green-on-darker-green golf courses—the sheer emerald beauty of Oregon—while the announcer, with a slight change in tone, says ". . . so that all summer and fall, tourists here can endure all of this [birds chirping, surfers laughing]."

Position is a passive noun: It's something the market does to you. You can try to influence your position. Or, like the state of Oregon in this example, you can take your position and turn it to your benefit.

No marketer ever followed this principle, "Take your position and turn it to your benefit," as brilliantly as Avis Rent A Car. Lagging behind Hertz for years in the 1960s and early 1970s, and saddled with its second-place position, the company decided to make second best a more desirable position than first.

"We're Number Two," Avis ads repeated for years. "We try harder."

People believed it. Sales soared.

The people at Avis did not try to position the company. They knew the market had already done it for them. They simply made the absolute most of the position they had.

Don't start by positioning your service. Instead, leverage the position you have.

Creating Your Positioning Statement

Before you create a positioning statement, one warning: Don't confuse a position with a positioning statement.

A *position* (or statement of position) is a cold-hearted, no-nonsense statement of how you are perceived in the minds of prospects. It *is* your position.

A *positioning statement*, by contrast, states how you *wish* to be perceived. It is the core message you want to deliver in every medium, including elevators and airport waiting areas, to influence the perceptions of your service.

You can establish your positioning statement by answering the following questions:

Who: Who are you?

What: What business are you in?

For whom: What people do you serve?

What need: What are the special needs of the people you serve?

Against whom: With whom are you competing?

What's different: What makes you different from those competitors?

So: What's the benefit? What unique benefit does a client derive from your service?

To illustrate, take Bloomingdale's:

(Who): "Bloomingdale's

(What) are fashion-focused department stores
(For whom) for trend-conscious, upper-middle-class shoppers
(What need) looking for high-end products.
(Against whom) Unlike other department stores,
(What's different) Bloomingdale's provides unique merchandise in a theatrical setting
(so) that makes shopping entertaining."

This was the Bloomingdale's position for years. Rather than make its "What's different?" couture and high-end fashions (Bergdorf Goodman's niche), or even fashion at all, Bloomingdale's positioned itself based on the *experience* of going there.

You can find other models for creating your position statement. None work better than this.

Ask yourself these seven questions—and have seven good clear answers.

Creating Your Position Statement

A positioning statement describes what you want the world to think. A statement of position, by contrast, admits the truth.

For most services, this statement of position basically reads:

(Who) "John Doe Inc.

(What) is a small service company

(For whom) that serves smaller clients who want pretty good quality but cannot pay, or do not want to pay, for the services of a larger company.

(Against whom) Unlike its bigger and better-known competitors,

(What's different) John Doe is smaller, less experienced, and not as outstanding, [Remember, this is the typical prospect's perception, and not necessarily reality.]

(So) but because of that, they charge less, so you can save some money."

This is the position of 90 percent of all service companies, because this is how they are perceived by potential customers.

Chances are that this, or some slightly improved version, is your position statement. This is where you must start.

So ask yourself, your clients, and your prospects, "What is our position?"

*Your position is all in people's minds. Find out what that position is.** *

*For this model and his strong influence on my thinking on positioning, I am again grateful to my old family friend Geoffrey Moore. Geoffrey is one of the four thinkers emeritus on high-tech marketing—William Davidow, Guy Kawasaki, and Regis McKenna being the other three—and his books contain excellent lessons for all marketers.

How to Narrow the Gap between Your Position and Your Positioning Statement

Getting prospects to move from how they see you—your position—to how you wish them to see you—the perception captured in your positioning statement—may require a huge push. And the wider the gap between your position and your statement, the stronger you must push.

Ask yourself: Given our position, will people *believe* our positioning statement?

This problem often arises when a small or midsized service tries to pitch that it is the "premier provider" of its service. Few prospects can reconcile "small or midsized" with "premier provider"; the claim fails the laugh test.

A similar problem occurs when a service with a well-entrenched position creates a new positioning statement that does not fit its established position. Take this frequent case in retailing:

Milt Franklin starts off in bowling supplies. He calls his company All Star Bowling; prospects position Milt as a bowling-supply provider.

Slowly, Milt learns that bowling supplies barely cover his overhead. So he adds golf supplies—even though bowlers and golfers are continents apart demographically, and even though few golfers would believe a bowling-supply salesman knows Tommy Armour 845s from Colt 45s.

Having diversified, Milt tacks onto All Star Bowling a new theme line, "Bowling, and a whole lot more." (These "And a whole lot more" themes, which abound in America, are a sure sign that the store owner has made a positioning mistake.)

Clients like Milt often name themselves into these problems, and then try to rename their way back out—something to consider before you call your restaurant Harry's Hoagies, say. But the Anchoring Principle warns you: Most people get anchored to your initial position and will not accept the new position if the gap between them is too wide.

In positioning, you have to jump from lily pad to nearby lily pad, one at a time.

If the gap between your position and your positioning statement is too big, your customers won't make the leap. Keep your steps small.

If That Isn't Our Positioning Statement, What Is It?

A too grand, overly bold positioning statement that tries to leap over too many lily pads still has value. It can be, and probably is, your *goal*.

Keep it. It can motivate your people, define your

longer-term goals, and guide your mission statement and long-term plan. It gives you an end in mind, as Stephen Covey puts it—a significant step toward being more effective.

Just because your statement is too grandiose for now doesn't mean you can't hope and try. But marketing must deal realistically with perceptions, and with the fact that people cannot make huge perceptual leaps. They can only make little jumps.

Have big goals and great visions—"big hairy audacious goals," as one writer put it. But make sure they are goals and visions—and not positioning statements.

Craft bold dreams and realistic positioning statements.

Repositioning Your Competitors

The country's top architects know how to design a position. They develop a style and then stand for it. They don't do some of this and some of that.

If you want avant-garde, you call Frank Gehry.

If you want postmodern wit, you call Michael Graves.

If you want very corporate late modern, you call I. M. Pei.

These architects "own" those positions. As a result, they own many other things, too.

Almost fifteen years ago, I saw Michael Graves's brilliant presentation to the City of Portland, Oregon, of his proposal for a new city hall. Graves immediately redefined the competition with his design and his manner. (His ingenious model included people sunbathing and jaywalking, and other humorous touches that got people to study the model closely.) His position veered so far from the others' that he made the others appear almost identical to one another, thus reducing the five-firm competition to two firms: Graves's and the best of the other four.

Graves did more than position himself. He also effectively repositioned his competitors. Suddenly they all appeared competent, but uninspired.

Once Graves had put himself in the finals, he moved to the middle—not unlike the political candidate who stakes a slightly extreme position in the primaries and then moves to the middle in the general election. Graves allayed some councilmembers' fears that he would go too far. That pink wouldn't really be *that* pink, they learned. Those wild ribbons cascading down the side of the building—well, maybe they wouldn't appear after all.

Graves won, and created a historic piece of architecture.

But before that, he created a very shrewd piece of positioning.

Choose a position that will reposition your competitors; then move a step back toward the middle to cinch the sale.

Positioning a Small Service

You are what you are.

You cannot try to be something that does not fit the way your prospects position you.

This is often painfully true in the most common service in this country: the small service company.

Prospects for these services—companies with from one to twenty employees generally—take the one thing they know about the service—its small size—and draw inferences.

Unfortunately, most of these inferences are negative: Why aren't you bigger? Why have I never heard of you before? Why aren't you working in a company I *have* heard of?

Some service companies do not recognize this problem, and they tilt at windmills. They try to hide their size or ignore the prospect's concern about it. These companies describe their service as second to none, when the prospect's clear perception is that the company is no better than fifth to many.

The small service must start with smallness—just as Oregon started with rain and Avis started with Number Two—and turn it into a positive.

The small service must start with small. It must dance with the one that brung it.

In positioning, don't try to hide your small size. Make it work by stressing its advantages, such as responsiveness and individual attention.

Focus: What Sears May Have Learned

If you are old enough to remember when bankers were the big shots in every town and when Univac was the world's most famous computer, you also remember when Sears was America's Department Store.

Years later, bankers have been the victims of inertia, Univac is a memory, and Sears is a near-casualty of the focus wars in department stores.

Amazingly, even while Americans seem more interested in austerity, Neiman Marcus appears to be thriving, thanks to a position that can best be described, as a Neiman's shopper might, as the purveyor of "Stuff *to die for!*" Wal-Mart is the terror of every small-town retailer, thanks to an equally clear focus on "Good stuff so damn cheap you won't believe it." And Bloomingdale's, while not the supernova it was in the eighties, still attracts a good business by focusing on "Shopping as entertainment."

Sears, in the first half of the 1990s, on the other hand, became the victim of focusing on nothing—or more accurately, on everything. Sears had always touted its high quality (but horribly low margin), durable goods such as lawn mowers. Now Sears started stressing its "softer side," its clothing and linens—a difficult marketing combination.

Sears started with very low prices. Then, hoping

to improve margins and attract what executives thought was a growing and lasting supply of cost-be-damned Yuppies, they tried to move prices up. Sears tried a little of this and a little of that—and in the middle of the decade, no American within two blocks of the Sears Tower could describe Sears's position. And if no prospect can describe your position, you do not have one.

Sears quickly discovered that if you do not have a focus, you soon might not have a business. Sales and profits plummeted. The store put its famous tower on the market and moved to more affordable quarters. All that made Sears tolerable to its share-holders were the corporation's Repair Centers, All-State Insurance, the Discover Card, and the underly-ing value of the company's real holdings.

In late 1995, however, the stores showed signs of rallying. By December 1995 same-store sales increased almost six percent despite a sluggish retail economy. Sears's major weapon in the rebound was an intense focus on the store's "softer side." Executives decided to let the impressive word of mouth for Sears's durable goods drive that portion of its business. They moved furniture out into separate free-standing furniture stores. Then, with aggressive "softer side" advertising, the addition of more nation-al clothing brands, wider aisles, softer lighting, and fancier displays, they drove up women's clothing sales 10 percent—an important improvement for a chain in which women make more than 70 percent of the purchases.

At this writing, it appears that Sears's focus on the softer and higher margin portion of its business might revive the stores. (Though one could also argue that Sears owns a unique "one-stop shopping" niche that has great appeal in this age of time-strapped consumers.)

In any case, if Sears had not found this focus, this section would not be subtitled "What Sears May Have Learned." It would be titled "Remember Sears?"

If you think you can afford not to focus, think of Sears.

Focus and the Clinton Campaign

He was dying. Bill Clinton had taken too many blows in the 1992 Democratic presidential primaries. Almost everyone involved with the campaign thought the end was near.

Clinton's problem was not his alleged fondness for women other than Hillary Clinton. It was his apparent fondness for chaos. He gave a speech one night and another the next, with no common themes.

Midway through the campaign, however, and with one dramatic gesture at a blackboard in Clinton's headquarters, campaign manager James Carville turned Clinton's entire campaign around with four words: "It's the Economy, Stupid."

From that moment the campaign rarely lost this focus. Before, his campaign speeches touched on everything from subsections of the tax code to escalator clauses in the Social Security laws. Now, Clinton hammered on the economy repeatedly. And eventually he hammered that message right through George Bush's heart.

Clinton aimed at the core of Americans—their historic materialism and their fears in the middle of a long recession—and repeatedly spoke to them. He became the economy candidate, the one who would address that problem. And despite all the rumors and all the suspicions, despite a controversial wife and a style that caused many people to mistrust him and dub him Slick Willy, Clinton won. Focus won.

Focus. In everything from campaigns for peanuts to campaigns for president, focus wins.

When the Banker's Eyes Blurred: Citicorp's Slip

If innovation drove Citicorp to the top, a lack of focus almost knocked it all the way back down.

In the 1980s, Citicorp resembled an overpaid and overpraised athlete who had read too many press clippings. The company's enormous success, fueled by its string of innovations, apparently convinced the people in the corner offices that Citicorp was above a fundamental principle of marketing: It did not have to focus. It could reach out everywhere and dominate the landscape, from high-volume consumer banking to global merchant banking.

At the same time, however, several banks got the focus religion. Bank of America left overseas and wholesale branches of banking to focus on becoming the dominant consumer bank on the West Coast. Chemical Bank moved out of international banking to focus on a large available niche: the middle-market and small-business customer.

Citicorp continued to stumble; it became a case study in stumbling, in loss of focus, in overreaching.

At this writing, the company's survival seems likely, if only because Citicorp now appears to have a focus: on the low-cost, high-volume niche of consumer banking. But the company's rise, stumble, and survival from its fall suggest this lesson:

No one—not even the most innovative and remarkable company in its industry—can be many things to many people.

No matter how skilled you are, you must focus your skills.

What Else Positions and Focus Can Do for You

They will make your word of mouth more effective. Instead of passing on the word that you are a marine service contract company, for example, people will be more apt to say you are America's *original* marine service contract company—a much more powerful position to boat owners who want their service contract provider around two years from now, when the lower unit on their boat engine blows up.

They will make your "word of elevator" more effective. Employees can be effective marketers just riding up the elevator—particularly if they have something powerful to say about your company. The reverse, unfortunately, also is true: Employees can hurt you if they do not know what makes your company special. When someone asks your uncertain employee about your company, and the employee gives a vague reply, the person often will interpret that response as indifference—and no one wants a service company with indifferent employees.

They can rally your troops. A message that conveys what makes your company special also can make employees feel special, simply by being part of your company.

They will get your marketing communications— and the people who create them—working as one. A clear position and focus gives everyone marching orders. The people behind your direct marketing, telemarketing, and advertising will know what to emphasize. People exposed to your message will see a common face and hear a common tune. They will learn exactly who you are.

Ugly Cats,
Boat Shoes, and
Overpriced Jewelry:
Pricing

Ugly Cats, Boat Shoes, and Overpriced Jewelry: The Sheer Illogic of Pricing

A Denver woman needed to sell four reasonably cute cats. She placed this classified ad in the *Denver Post:*

"Ugly Cats. $100 each. 555-5555."

More than eighty people called. She said she could have sold the cats for far more.

Timberland was struggling in the early 1980s. The company made a good boat-type shoe and priced it below the leader, Topsiders. A great product for the price—but not a good business. Then Timberland did something fairly simple: It increased its price to be well above Topsiders.

Sales boomed—just as they boomed for American Express when it took over the prestige niche in credit cards by pricing its card just one dollar more than a Diners Club card.

In *Influence*, Robert Cialdini tells about the frustrated owner of a Native American jewelry store in Arizona. The owner had not been able to sell some turquoise jewelry, even though it was peak tourist season. She tried sales. Nothing. She tried sales "training" (she encouraged her staff to push the jewelry). Nothing.

Finally, the night before she was leaving for a trip,

the owner left her head saleswoman a note: "Everything in this display case, price × ½."

The owner returned a few days later and learned that everything had sold—but not for the reason she thought. The saleswoman had misread the owner's scribbled note to read "price × 2," and *doubled* the price of everything!

Some people think pricing is one of the more logical acts of marketing. These examples say something different.

Don't assume that logical pricing is smart pricing. Maybe your price, which makes you look like a good value, actually makes you look second-rate.

Pricing: The Resistance Principle

Just months into business, I have made my first great discovery about business," a young woman recently told me. "There's one simple way to get all the business you can handle: Charge almost nothing."

She's right.

If no one complains about your price, it's too low.

If almost everyone complains, it's too high.

So if no price resistance is too low and 100 percent is too high, how much resistance is just right? How much resistance tells you that your price is right?

Fifteen to 20 percent. And there is one simple reason why: Close to 10 percent of people will complain about any price. Some want a deal. Others are
mistrustful and assume every price is overstated. Still
others want to get the price they had in their mind
when they approached you, because it's the price
they hoped for and already have budgeted in their
mind.

So throw out the group that will object no matter
what your price Then ask: In the remaining cases,
how often do I encounter resistance?

Resistance in 10 percent of those remaining
cases—for a total of almost 20 percent—is about
right. When it starts exceeding 25 percent, scale
back.

***Setting your price is like setting a screw. A little
resistance is a good sign.***

Avoiding the
Deadly Middle

Companies in many services essentially set their
rates by studying the going, high, and low rates, and
then deciding where they fall on the quality spec-
trum. This unfortunate practice tells their customers
exactly how good the company *really* thinks it is.

Ask yourself: If that's how you are pricing your

services, what are you saying to your customers and prospects—that you aren't that great?

Another problem with this pricing strategy is the Problem of the Deadly Middle. If you are the high-priced provider, most people assume you offer the best quality—a desirable position. If you are the low-cost provider, most people assume you deliver an acceptable product at the lowest cost—also a desirable position. But if you price in the middle, what you are saying—again—is: "We're not the best, and neither is our price, but both our service and price are pretty good." Not a very compelling message.

The premium service and the low-cost provider occupy nice niches all by themselves. If you are priced in between, however, you are competing with almost everyone. And that's a lot of everyones.

Beware of the Deadly Middle.

The Low-Cost Trap

You can make a good marketing case for becoming the low-cost provider.

Your position is clear and so is your price; it's the lowest a prospect can find.

But the low-cost position kills.

Where are they now, the great low-priced services of our past? The old synonyms for low-cost retailing—such as J.C. Penney, Montgomery Ward, and

Sears—are dead, dying, or reeling. At this writing, five discounters in the Northeast alone are suffering even more. Caldor and Bradlees have filed for bankruptcy, Jamesway is considering it, and Ames and Filene's are bleeding red ink.

Low-cost providers take it from several directions. Cutting costs requires little imagination, and the low-cost position can be seized without a large investment in brand building. So in most nonretail service industries, the low-cost provider is a relatively easy market niche to enter. Just when you perfect your system for reducing costs, someone else devises a better one—as discount retailers discovered when Wal-Mart jumped in.

Many low-cost providers attain their position through ruthless dealing with suppliers. Over the short term, that squeezing can work; suppliers who need the business grudgingly oblige. But those suppliers never become allies. They even may generate bad word-of-mouth to compensate for the bad treatment they receive. If those suppliers get a good chance to get out of the deal years later, they do— gleefully, bad word-of-mouth trailing them as they flee.*

Cost shavers also find it harder to inspire employees. Employees often see a company's intelligent austerity as mean-spirited cheapness. Would you like a windowless, carpetless cubicle forty-five hours a

---

*For a detailed view of the extraordinary value of good supplier relationships in a service, see *McDonald's: Behind the Arches* by John Love. This book could change how you view all the different stakeholders in your company and how you approach your marketing.

week—or a leather chair that revolves around to reveal the view out your window?

But this is soft thinking, you say. Where's the hard data suggesting that low cost is a trap?

In the *Harvard Business Review.* In its September–October 1980 issue, William Hull reported his study comparing companies that stressed differentiation with companies that competed on cost.

In every measure that mattered—in return on equity, return on capital, and average annual revenue growth rate—the differentiators beat the tightwads every time.

Hull's study echoed what the people at ADP, the country's leader in payroll processing, have discovered. "We will never try to develop a strategy based on pricing," CEO Josh Weston had said. "There is *nothing* unique about pricing."

Remember this: Most service prospects can find an even lower cost option than yours; they can do the service themselves or not at all. The homeowner can paint his own house or postpone it indefinitely; the woman with a troublesome mole can diagnose her own ailment or refuse medical service altogether; the aggrieved subcontractor can take his own case to court or say to hell with it.

People almost always can find a cheaper way to get your service—and few efforts are less rewarding than trying to compete with those cheaper ways.

Beware of the rock bottom.

Pricing: A Lesson from Picasso

In many services—overnight delivery, dry cleaning, fast foods—the "product" of the service has become a commodity, and commodity pricing rules prevail: To the low-priced go the spoils.

But in millions of other services, pricing is a not-so-simple matter of "What Will the Market Bear?"

A lot, it often seems. A friend marvels at his older brother, who earns a million dollars a year telling companies like Coca-Cola what the future might be. Lawrence Tribe charges $750 an hour to read, think, and occasionally argue cases before the Supreme Court. Film directors, great photographers, top consultants, and many others charge enough to buy Monets.

What *is* talent and thought worth—and why is some worth so much? What can you reasonably charge? Good questions. Before you answer them, consider this story about Pablo Picasso:

A woman was strolling along a street in Paris when she spotted Picasso sketching at a sidewalk café. Not so thrilled that she could not be slightly presumptuous, the woman asked Picasso if he might sketch her, and charge accordingly.

Picasso obliged. In just minutes, there she was: an original Picasso.

"And what do I owe you?" she asked.

"Five thousand francs," he answered.

"But it only took you three minutes," she politely reminded him.

"No," Picasso said. "It took me all my life."

Don't charge by the hour. Charge by the years.

The Carpenter Corollary to the Picasso Principle

A man was suffering a persistent problem with his house. The floor squeaked. No matter what he tried, nothing worked. Finally, he called a carpenter who friends said was a true craftsman.

The craftsman walked into the room and heard the squeak. He set down his toolbox, pulled out a hammer and nail, and pounded the nail into the floor with three blows.

The squeak was gone forever. The carpenter pulled out an invoice slip, on which he wrote the total of $45. Above that total were two line items:

Hammering, $2.

Knowing where to hammer, $43.

Charge for knowing where.

Value Is Not a Position

If your primary selling position is good value, you have no position.

Value is not a competitive position. Value is what every service promises, implicitly or explicitly. It is fundamental to survival. A service's price *must* fairly reflect its value to the customer, or the service eventually will fail.

Some legal services charge $50 for an uncontested divorce. Lawyer Lawrence Tribe charges $750 an hour. Acme's clients say they get good value, and most clients and experts point to Tribe's results—a 15–6 winning record before the U.S. Supreme Court—and they say he gives very good value, too.

In services, value is a given. And givens are *not* viable competitive positions.

If good value is the first thing you communicate, you won't be effective.

If good value is your best position, improve your service.

MONOGRAM YOUR SHIRTS, NOT YOUR COMPANY: NAMING AND BRANDING

Monogram Your Shirts, Not Your Company

ADP DMM ETI ADC APC ABC CBC BCW
Which "name" above did you remember?
None?
Don't worry. *Everyone* flunks that memory test.

It's because people cannot remember monograms. Monograms have no memorability. Just as bad, monograms have no spirit, no attitude, no message, no promise, no warmth, and no humanity.

So why do so many companies use monograms?

Blame IBM. IBM convinced executives that if they gave their company a fancy monogram like IBM, they would succeed like IBM.

This is like thinking that Michael Jordan's shoes will make you like Mike.

It's also like thinking that dinner causes midnight, because midnight always comes after dinner.

Dinners don't cause midnight. And IBM's name didn't cause IBM's success.

Give your service a name, not a monogram.

Don't Make Me Laugh

It's tempting to create a clever name.

Sometimes, this temptation becomes so strong that you give your service a slightly funny name. Let's say, Hair Apparent for a hair transplant clinic.

Here's a test that will talk you out of this mistake.

Look up one of those wittily named services (chances are it's a hair salon or a pizza place). Go there and go in. You will notice two things:

You have never been there before.

And it's almost empty.

Don't get funny with your name.

To Stand Out, Stand Out

Kimberly-Clark spends millions of dollar a year keeping people from calling tissues kleenexes. Xerox does the same to keep the word "Xerox" from becoming a synonym for "photocopy."

Why the fuss? Because these companies do not want their name to become generic. They want their name to stand for *their* product.

Just as sophisticated marketers do not want their brand names to become generic, you do not want a generic name as your brand. A generic name is not your name; it is everyone's.

Three Twin Cities companies call themselves Financial Services Inc., Financial Specialists Inc., and Financial Counseling Inc. If someone from Financial Specialists called you, isn't there a great chance that months later you might think that call came from Financial Services?

Do you want people *not* to know who you are? Not to remember you? Not to be impressed by you immediately? Not to be able to tell your company from half a dozen others?

Generic names encourage generic business.

Tell Me Something I Don't Know

Among advertising people, it is assumed that companies named Creative (Something) are *not* creative.

That's partly because a name like Creative Design contradicts itself. The name, after all, could not be less creative.

The same is true of Quality, as in Quality Cleaners. Doesn't that sound like a cleaner that might break your buttons?

Never choose a name that describes something that everyone expects from the service. The name will be generic, forgettable, and meaningless.

Distinctive Position, Distinctive Name

What does the brain remember best?

The authors of *Brain Book* answered this. They studied human memory and concluded that the mind best remembers things that are "*unique*, sensory, creative, and *outstanding*."

Advocates of distinctive names argue that distinctive names are more apt to be remembered—and being remembered often is the key to getting business.

But another argument for distinctive names rests on a basic principle of successful marketing: Make yourself different.

The human mind associates. When we hear ordinary names like John Jones we draw an ordinary association. When we hear distinctive names like Faith Popcorn or Leaf Phoenix, we draw distinctive associations.

An ordinary name implies just another service. A distinctive name implies a distinctive service—just the impression a service should make.

In a world filled with me-too company names, service companies with distinctive names like NameLab, Federal Express, and Prodigy quickly create the association that they are *not* me-too services—and profit from the association.

Be distinctive—and sound it.

What's in a Name?

What if LeAnn Chin's restaurant was called Beijing?

Would LeAnn Chin have made the cover of almost every magazine in Minnesota?

No. By naming her restaurant LeAnn Chin, she ensured that every mention of herself was an ad for her restaurant, and vice versa.

By naming her restaurant after herself, LeAnn Chin made herself a celebrity. Her celebrity made the restaurant more popular. So she started a chain of restaurants. The restaurants' increasing popularity made her more of a celebrity, which made the restaurants even more popular, and on and on—in a not at all vicious circle.

If you need a name for your service, start with your own.

Names: The Information-per-Inch Test

Why do many *Fortune* 500 companies pay over $35,000 for a name?

Because names make a company's first impression. First impressions count—and often convey much of the little information about you that your prospects have.

Given what a good name is worth, how do you measure a name's value?

Put the name to this test: *How much valuable information per inch does your name imply?*

A wonderfully named San Francisco company perfectly illustrates the Information-per-Inch Principle—and given its business, it should. The company is NameLab—a company that specializes in naming products.

With lightning speed, NameLab's name suggests the company takes a near-scientific, analytic approach to developing names, something distinct in its industry. Beyond that, the freshness and slight whimsy of the name NameLab also suggests the company's capacity for creative, right-brain thinking. So NameLab conveys a powerful double meaning to its prospects, with an excellent information-per-inch ratio.

Ask yourself: If you needed a good name for your service, whom would you call first? Names Inc., The Name Company, or NameLab?

If you were a journalist writing a story on product or service names, which company would you call first? (So far, every journalist's answer has been NameLab, as you may have noticed in dozens of publications.)

A week later, which company's name would you remember?

And when that time came to name your company, which company would you probably call for help?

Give every name you consider the Information-per-Inch Test.

The Cleverness of Federal Express

The master packer of naming—the company that may have squeezed more good information into each inch of its name—is Federal Express.

"Express" was not being widely used when Fred Smith chose Federal Express's name. Thanks to its usage in Pony Express and other places, "Express" connotes "rapid mail delivery"—faster than conventional mail.

Now came the company's next question: What else should our name communicate? "Nationwide," they agreed. Quickly, Smith probably considered the names National Express, Nationwide Express, and US Express—the obvious names that come quickly to mind.

By contrast, "federal," a legalistic term for a political system of states with a central government, does not come quickly to mind—a great asset in a name. To give the name even more impact in the company's competition with government postal services, "federal" also connotes an official government sanction or status. (Smith admitted that he liked "Federal" because it sounded patriotic, although his main reason for fixing on "Federal" was that his initial business plan called for his company to deliver air freight for the Federal Reserve.)

So Federal is a more distinctive, more memorable, and more authoritative way to convey "nationwide."

Now look at Federal Express in color. The colors again hint at the government-sanctioned theme with their twist on red, white, and blue, but connote better quality by replacing the government's ordinary blue with a richer purple-blue.

So Federal Express conveys a distinctive and powerful message—"like the US mail, only faster and better"—in just two words and two colors—a *terrific* information-per-inch ratio.

Use Federal Express as your standard, and ask: How much does your name communicate, how fast? Are you using color effectively? Is it conveying the same message as your name?

The Brand Rush

A revealing week in my life:

Monday, a gifted lawyer calls. He quickly explains his problem. He is among the premier practitioners in his specialty, but he is losing business to inferior lawyers in two brand-name law firms. He wants that hole plugged.

Wednesday afternoon, the president of a contracting company calls. A heavily advertised competitor is charging far more for comparable jobs and still getting the bids, despite my caller's roomful of industry trophies.

Thursday morning, the president of a professional consulting firm calls. Her firm has grown incrementally by word of mouth, and cannot penetrate the more lucrative, challenging, and prestigious accounts that would give the firm more stature. The big-name firms own all those accounts.

This was an actual week in my life in 1995. By year's end I was ready to dub it The Year of the Brand Rush—the year when thousands of service companies finally realized the enormous clout of brands.

Each caller was getting beaten by a brand. Each caller's company offered demonstrably excellent, even superior service, yet each was losing business to brands. Each company was growing, but more sluggishly than it deserved.

But each executive had finally realized something critical:

In service marketing, almost nothing beats a brand.

Aren't Brands Dying?

The business magazine headlines ask, "Are Brands Dead?" You see several of those headlines over time and decide the rumors must be true.

They aren't.

Those who argue that brands are dying offer as Exhibit One the rise of store-branded or generic products.

Those observers are overlooking something: Generic products are *not* truly non-branded. In a reputable store, the generic product carries a distinctive promise: the promise of the store. The store promises that the product will perform and that the store will back it. The generic product, in short, carries the store's brand.

Clearly, store-branded products have brands— service brands rather than product brands, but still brands. To the customer, the fact that the store is convenient and one with which the customer probably has dealt for years gives that store brand special power.

But just for argument, assume that generic and store-labeled products are not brands. Then what?

At this writing, store and generic brands own 7 percent of the market; name brands own the remaining 93 percent. Considering the much lower cost of generics and store brands, the heavy publicity about the high quality of many store brands, and the number of savvy consumers who realize that many store brands are simply name brands in store packaging, the fact that these store and generic brands still own only 7 percent of the market seems amazing—until you recognize the enormous power of a brand.

Name national brands charge substantially more—up to 40 percent more—for products that often only equal store products in quality. Yet name national brands still represent thirteen of every fourteen sales in the market. Amazing—and perhaps the best evidence of the enormous power of brands.

Brands are alive—and you could use one.

The Warranty of a Brand

What is a brand?

A brand is more than a symbol. In the public's eye, a brand is a *warranty*. It is a promise that the service carrying that brand will live up to its name, and perform.

A brand is even more important than a warranty. No warranty does enough, because no warranty compensates the warranty holder for the lost time, the frustration, and the inconvenience of suffering the problem and making the claim. The brand, then, becomes even more important because it is the closest thing to a guarantee that the customer will not need the warranty and have to endure the claims process.

Brands are even more important to service customers, because few services have warranties—in part because many services are very difficult to warrant. How do you warrant, for example, that legal advice will be good? That a waiter's service will be satisfactory? That a tax accountant will find every permissible deduction? In many cases, you cannot. Left without a warranty, the client has only the brand on which to depend.

And depending on brands is just what service clients do.

A service is a promise, and building a brand builds your promise.

The Heart of a Brand

When a prospect initially agrees to use a typical service, what does he own?

Nothing but someone's promise that they will do something.

The most desirable services, then, are those that keep their promises.

This also means that the heart of a service brand—the element without which the brand cannot live—is the integrity of the company and its employees.

The value of any brand rises or falls with each demonstration of the company's integrity. The balance is fragile; every slip can be costly. We all have worked with services that failed us only once, but fatally. They lied or came close. From that one experience, their brand lost all its value to us. When others later asked us about that company, we may have said very little, but our message was clear—and it spread.

A service can be faster, cheaper, better, and still fail if it does not win the confidence of people that it will keep its promises and tell the truth.

The heart of a service brand is not artful packaging, slick advertising, or the company name emblazoned on everything from sweatshirts to key chains. The heart of a service brand, and a key to a service's long-term success, is the integrity of the people behind it.

Invest in and religiously preach integrity. It is the heart of your brand.

What Brands Do for Sales

A brand will have three dramatic effects on your selling:

First, consider a common occurrence. Someone hears a positive story about a nonbranded company. They remember the story but naturally forget the company's name. So they cannot pass the story on. When the same person hears a story about a brand-name service, he remembers the story and the company. So he can pass the story along—and does. Word of mouth for a branded service spreads easier and farther, producing more inquiries.

Second, a brand singlehandedly converts more of these inquiries into clients. Prospects feel more comfortable—and less fearful—with a brand name. "No one ever got fired for choosing IBM," the old saw goes. It applies to choosing brand-name services, too. For the same amount of selling effort, a branded service makes more sales than a nonbranded service.

Third, consider the plight of the typical nonbranded service. To justify her choice of a nonbranded service, a prospective client often must schedule follow-up presentations with the key people in her company (or her spouse, if it is a consumer service). Frequently, a nonbranded service will spend more on this lengthy selling process than the initial project is worth. Branded services rarely face that expense. In fact, prospects routinely choose brand-name services virtually sight unseen, so brands take less time and expense to sell.

Brand-name services can spend less time and money to get more business. This gives them greater profits to reinvest to make their company even more productive—and widen the gulf between them and their nonbranded competitors.

Make selling easier, faster, and cheaper. Build a brand.

Stand by Your Brand

It is *the* tale of the wild world of advertising, per-haps—but the moral often is missed.

A hot ad agency emerges. It wins dozens of awards and the adoration of a hungry trade press looking for the newest thing. Eventually, the hot agency wins a big account. If it is good and lucky, the agency keeps that account and wins even more. It becomes a brand.

Almost everyone is happy. Everyone except George, Ed, Mary, and Nancy—the team who did all the work for which their agency is taking credit. Flush with confidence, the foursome meet secretly and make a decision. They will haul their Clios, their clippings, and their prodigious talent to a neat loft downtown and build their own hot agency.

Remember that George, Ed, Mary, and Nancy comprise the entire team—the account person, media planner, writer, and art director—who created those fabulous commercials that made the hot agency hot. They are the people that Coca-Cola trusted with $60 million.

Does this tale end with our four heroes living happily ever after? Sadly, no. Their new agency gets a nice assignment here and there, but for years, they struggle with tight budgets, fewer clippings, and a growing sense that something is missing.

What has happened? George, Ed, Mary, and

Nancy still have the talent and experience—*but they no longer have the brand.*

All they have lost is their brand. But the loss is enormous.

The four struggle on, thinking that prospective clients will see through the sheer folly of this brand thing and recognize that GEM&N are really their old brand agency under a new roof—and with much lower overhead to boot.

And then one Friday, George locks GEM&N's doors behind him for the last time.

GEM&N were not beaten by bad planning, the sudden disappearance of their muses, or a U-turn in the economy. They were beaten by a brand—the one they lost and never regained.

Never underestimate the value of your brand or the difficulty in creating a new one.

The Four-Hundred-Grand Brand

Here's a true story, with the names changed to protect the innocent and the fortunate.

Two men, Phil and Don, spent seven years building a contracting company into a solid business. They aren't famous, but they do well enough to order filet mignons without thinking twice. In 1995, another man approached them and offered $400,000 for their business.

Phil and Don's contracting company had no inventory, no proprietary products or services, no patents or copyrights, and only one employee other than Phil and Don. The company rented a storefront and owned no real estate, no capital assets, and no accounts receivable. A thorough accounting, in fact, would have revealed that the $400,000 company's only assets were its name and client list.

What was the buyer offering to buy?

Was it the client list? It couldn't be. Clients used the company's service only once or twice in a lifetime. Repeat business wasn't much better than in funeral parlors. Moreover, the client list had value only if the clients thought that although the old owners were no longer with the company, the company would still provide the same high quality.

In other words, those old clients—and any new ones—were simply buying the brand. And that is what the businessman offered $400,000 for, too: a $400,000 brand, built in just seven years with relatively little investment.

For years, AMRE, a Dallas-based provider of vinyl siding, paid Sears $30 million *each* year—more than seven times AMRE's net profit—to license Sears's brand name. As a result, and because of the consumer's confidence in the Sears name, AMRE was able to mark up each siding sale 2.2 times—far over industry norms. (In 1995, AMRE realized there was a good brand with a much lower price and struck a twenty-year, $230 million licensing agreement with Century 21.)

Kraft sold for eight times its book value. Experts agreed that the only explanation was the enduring power and enormous value of the Kraft brand.

What is a brand worth? Should you try to build one?

Thousands, millions, then billions. And emphatically, yes.

A brand is money.

Brands in a Microwave World

You want a new sound system. Because you love music and hate wasting money on large purchases, you want to choose wisely. But you also have eight calls to return, a lawn to mow, one recital, and three Little League practices—you are, in short, the typical Got-No-Time American.

You cannot buy more time, so you must give some up. You need shortcuts. You need some way to speed your decision on that sound system.

Fortunately, you find your shortcut: a brand-name system.

Brands are decision-making shortcuts in a world of people like you looking for shortcuts. Often, a brand is all the information some people will need to choose their next sound system—even though at least one unbranded system is clearly superior and 30 percent cheaper than the system they choose.

In choosing a brand-name sound system, you demonstrate a rule of modern marketing: As time shrinks, the importance of brands increases. And time in America *is* shrinking; companies have downsized their staffs and upsized the workloads of all the survivors. These people need shortcuts every waking minute. They turn to service and product brands.

Give your prospects a shortcut. Give them a brand.

Brands and the Power of the Unusual

Try this test:

The following are most of the great brand names of the English-speaking world (a few brands have been overlooked, although being overlooked says something about that brand):

Harley Davidson	Sony	Honda
Procter & Gamble	Nike	Levi Strauss
Rolls Royce	Disney	
Xerox Kleenex	Coca-Cola	Mercedes-Benz
Lloyd's of London	Nikon	
Harvard Kodak	Microsoft	Marlboro

What is striking about this list? It is how *unusual* these names are. *Virtually no one or nothing else carries any of these names.* You know no other Sony, Disney, Harvard, Kodak, or Harley. Unless you studied mythology and recognize the goddess Nike, or studied anthropology and remember Claude Lévi-Strauss, you have no other connotations for Nike and Levi Strauss, either.

Consider the brand names in the following services, and ask yourself: Where else have you heard these names?

Accounting: Ernst & Young, Deloitte Touche, Coopers & Lybrand, Peat Marwick.

Law: Skadden & Arps, Covington & Burling, Fulbright & Jaworski, Pillsbury, Madison & Sutro.

Consulting and consultants: McKinsey, Bain, Senge, Hamel, Prahalad, Drucker.

Business schools: Wharton, Tuck, Fuqua, Harvard, Stanford.

Granted, in each of these four service categories you find one "usual" name: Arthur Andersen in accounting, Sullivan & Cromwell in law, Tom Peters in consulting, and Kellogg in business schools. (Although giving a business school the name of a successful and well-regarded business sounds like smart marketing, even if the name is not unusual.)

But each of these exceptions seems to prove the rule.

Most of the great brand names are *unconfusable:* People associate those brand names only with the companies behind them. The names have no bad associations created by their connection to something else with the same name.

We follow this principle when we name our children. We ruthlessly exclude every name with any negative association. So after Nixon and Watergate, Americans stopped naming boys Richard, just as parents everywhere stopped naming children Adolf after World War II.

People's minds are quick to make connotations. The smart service company avoids any rub-off of negative connotations by developing unconfusable brand names.

To speed up the building of your brand, choose an unconfusable name.

Brands and the Baby-sitter

Brands are for the rich, you say.

Not so—as the story of the baby-sitter shows.

Kate Thurman is the future president of a very successful company, but today, she is a high school freshman, a baby-sitter, and a born marketer. Kate seeks out every neighborhood place that parents frequent: the toy store, Gymboree storefront, day care centers, and school summer camps. She convinces proprietors they are serving parents by posting Kate's signs for her service, "KATE ♥ KIDS."

Borrowing the idea from local remodelers, Kate also creates a red, blue, and white sign: "KATE ♥ KIDS—World Class Babysitting: 555-1111" and mounts it on her old red-and-white rocking horse. On the lawn of every house where she sits, Kate plants the rocking horse.

Kate's uncle Frank owns the neighborhood video store—another marketing opportunity. Kate convinces Frank to let her place her red, white, and blue ad in the clear sleeves on the back of each video jacket. Kate pays for this with three free nights of baby-sitting for Frank's baby girl—whom Kate adores and would happily watch for free.

Kate then becomes a baby-sitter temp agency. She lines up other girls to work in return for 10 percent of their pay. Local parents know they will always get a sitter through Kate, so they are willing to pay Kate a 15 percent premium for eliminating their hassle of finding sitters, especially at the last minute. So Kate's employees make more per hour through Kate than they would earn on their own. Naturally, savvy local sitters start going through Kate.

Kate has created a dynasty. Everyone in her ten-square-mile neighborhood recognizes her name. When parents from other neighborhoods ask Sheridan residents about sitters, they say: "Call Kate." And those parents do.

The local press soon hears about the young entrepreneur and writes a story. A reporter for the local CBS affiliate reads the story, calls Kate, and does a three-minute feature on "WE ♥ KIDS" on the six o'clock news. Kate charms and impresses everyone listening—all 170,000 people.

In the entire market that she serves, Kate has built a booming brand.

For about $32 in paint and plywood.

Building your brand doesn't take millions. It takes imagination.

How to Save $500,000:
Communicating
and Selling

Communicating: A Preface

Because services are intangible, marketing communications for services do more than promote services. Communications make services more tangible, and give prospects something firm to evaluate.

As a result, marketing communications for most services haul around a heavier burden than communications for products. A bright red Porsche 911 convertible, for example, speaks—loudly and beautifully—for itself. Very few services speak for themselves at all.

We implicitly trust most products. We trust that our new tires won't blow out, our brown sugar will taste sweet, and our aspirin will soothe our headaches without bad side effects. But we are far less trusting and certain about most services.

We worry that our lawyers and auto mechanics will do more than necessary, and charge more than necessary. We worry that the latest weight-loss service will fail, just like the three before it. We worry that our remodelers will exceed their budget and finish weeks after they promise. We worry that the collection agency we hire for our service will harass our clients worth keeping and collect only a small part of our outstanding receivables.

So unlike communicating about products, communicating about services must make the service more tangible and real, and must soothe the worried prospect.

It's not like selling Porsche automobiles.

The first two rules of communicating about services: *Make the service visible, and make the prospect comfortable.*

Fran Lebowitz and Your Greatest Competitor

It's not a cold, hard world; it's just a very busy one. You know it firsthand: a dozen things compete for your attention, and you have only so much attention to give.

So you must know that your prospects have only so much attention to give, too. Give them powerful reasons to listen to you, or they will give you only ear service. They may listen, but they will not hear.

Your greatest competition is not your competition. It is *indifference.*

Many service marketers know this, but few act on it. Instead of talking about the prospect and what she needs, these marketers talk about their company. Instead of showing what they will do for a prospect, they strive to show how good their company is. Instead of speaking the prospect's language, they speak their own.

The prospect is thinking, "Me, me, me." Unfortunately, the marketer is thinking that, too. The two fail to connect.

Few people are particularly interested in what you have to say. (As Fran Lebowitz once said of people who wore sweatshirts with messages, "People don't want to hear from you—so what makes you think they want to hear from your shirt?") People are interested in *themselves*. Until you realize that, you will be beaten badly by your toughest competitor: indifference.

Your first competitor is indifference.

The Cocktail Party Phenomenon

Psychologists call it the Cocktail Party Phenomenon. (Psychologists, it appears, have learned the value of memorable packaging, too.) You've experienced the cocktail party phenomenon. It works like this:

You're listening to someone at a cocktail party. Suddenly, you hear your name mentioned in a nearby conversation. Now you can hear that conversation, but you no longer can hear the one in which you were involved.

This happens because people cannot process two conversations at once. If you deliver two messages, most people will process just one of them— if that.

Say one thing.

The Grocery List Problem

Actually, the challenge of getting your message across is greater than the Cocktail Party Phenomenon might suggest.

Consider this:

Mom sends you to the store for milk. You bring home the milk.

Next time, she says, "Get raisins, Drano, Gummy Bears, milk, and some hundred-watt light bulbs."

You forget the milk; but it's the milk your family needed most. All you have for breakfast tomorrow is cereal.

You run this risk when you hand prospects a grocery list of different messages about you. They remember the raisins, which aren't important, and forget the milk. Your prospects forget your real point of distinction, and remember a supporting message that hardly matters.

Now, consider some even grimmer evidence against communicating too much. Horace Schwerin and Henry Newell, in their helpful book *Persuasion*, described their test of two commercials for the same car. Commercial one was single-minded: It talked only about performance. Commercial two went further. It pointed out that in addition to exceptional performance, the car offered outstanding styling, a choice of several models, and excellent economy. (This type of commercial is known in the agency business as The Commercial the Client Will Love.)

After showing subjects the two commercials, the testers asked viewers if either commercial might make them switch to that brand of car. Six percent answered yes, the performance spot *would* make them consider switching.

But what about the second commercial, with all that valuable added information—how many were affected by it?

Not one. Zero percent.

Saying many things usually communicates nothing.

Give Me One Good Reason

You want the strongest argument for a single focused message? Ask your prospects.

Your prospects have one basic question: What makes you so different that I should do business with you?

Your prospects are making the classic statement: *Give me one good reason why.*

It's a simple request that begs for a simple response. A complex response will just give your prospect another problem to sort out. Your prospect does not want more to think about; your prospect wants *less.*

An example from retailing shows the importance of a simple message. Go to a good men's store like

Barney's in New York. Ask for a blue-striped oxford shirt. A savvy salesman will show you one nice shirt, which you probably will buy. But if he isn't that smart and shows you three shirts, there is an excellent chance you won't buy *any* shirt. The salesperson has complicated your decision and confused you with choices. And it is very hard to sell to a confused person.

Meet your market's very first need: Give it one good reason.

Your Favorite Songs

Driving down the freeway, you switch on your favorite radio station and hear a song for the first time. You like it but do not remember it.

The next afternoon you hear the song again. Perhaps you note the singer, and perhaps you remember her name.

Two mornings later, you hear the song again. After making sure no other commuters are watching, you start singing along with the hook, which you now remember.

Two days later you buy the CD. You play it several evenings. By the third evening, you know most of the words.

It has taken seven or eight playings for the song's message to sink in. But finally, it has.

What if the singer changed the song and tune every time? What would you remember?

Almost nothing.

What does this tell you about your marketing communications?

Can you keep changing your words, your melody, your entire theme?

If you do, what will people remember? For what will they know you?

After you say one thing, repeat it again and again.

One Story Beats a Dozen Adjectives

Pick up a good magazine and glance at a few stories.

You may spot a pattern that tells you something.

Today, most nonfiction writers begin their articles with an illustrative story. It's a device so pervasive there is a name for it: synecdoche.

Trial lawyer Gerry Spence almost always makes a point with a story. Spence knows that for all the enormous changes in Western culture since the Greeks, today, almost 2,500 years after Euripides, our primary form of entertainment is still the dramatic narrative—the *story.*

More marketers should discover the power of stories. Just as stories make articles more interesting and make Spence's arguments more persuasive, they make marketing communications more effective.

Synecdoche works because people are interested in other people, and stories are about people. Gerry Spence's story of a person wronged by excessive police force does not need the words "pain" and "injustice." His vivid story makes jurors *feel* the pain and injustice.

Like clever journalists and great lawyers, marketers who tell true stories make their presentations more interesting, more personal, more credible, and more felt—and more persuasive.

Don't use adjectives. Use stories.

Attack the Stereotype

Almost every well-known service suffers from a well-known stereotype.

Accountants are humorless.

Lawyers are greedy.

Collections agencies are bullies.

Doctors keep you waiting.

The stereotype of your service is the first thing that a prospect thinks about. It is the first hurdle you must jump, and the first one over usually wins.

Attack your first weakness: the stereotype the prospect has about you.

Don't Say It, Prove It

Carolyn Adams, then circulation director of the *Utne Reader*, once sent me the magazine's subscription solicitation letters for the past ten years. She said they never had written a letter that could outperform the first one, written by a famous copywriter.

The first letter was the best example of good, readable writing. It was specific, not general. It was concrete, not abstract. It used vivid and familiar examples to make its points. The last sentence of each paragraph enticed you to read the first sentence of the next. The writer never used two words when one would do.

The difference in this letter wasn't direct-marketing gimmicks and tricks. It wasn't the teaser headline on the envelope; it didn't have one. It wasn't the shrewd use of the P.S.; it didn't have one of those, either.

This letter was just good communication. It never said that the *Utne Reader* was great. It skipped all those adjectives and all the puffing, and proved it: This was a very interesting magazine and well worth the price.

Good basic communicating is good basic marketing.

Build Your Case

In the last three years, three of my clients have offered the best service in their entire industry. But do their prospects know it?

Thousands of them didn't know. And puffery would never have convinced them.

So two of the clients commissioned independent customer satisfaction surveys. The scores were astonishing. So they told their prospects.

In one case, they told their prospects that the company had received the highest customer satisfaction scores an independent surveying firm had ever recorded.

In the other, the company asked the respondents to score the client. The company then translated these customer satisfaction scores into grade point averages based on the traditional 4.0 scales. The company's service quality score was a fabulous 3.96.

They built their case.

Merely saying you offer great service will never work. You have to document and demonstrate it.

Create the evidence of your service quality. Then communicate it.

Tricks Are for Kids

A service is a promise. You're selling the promise that at some future date, you will do something.

This means what you really are selling is your honesty.

Tricks and gimmicks aren't honest.

Gimmicky headlines, swimsuit models, direct marketing tricks—they're all a form of bait and switch.

And these tricks say one thing. They tell your prospects you are willing to trick them.

And that tells your prospects that you'll try to trick them again.

Don't.

*No **tricks**.*

The Joke's on You

A friend tells you a lame joke.

You laugh, of course. It's human nature.

You send someone what you think is a clever gimmick promotion—let's say, a plastic fish with a note inside: "Let's hook up. We're a great catch," or something (heaven help you) better.

You call to ask your prospect if she received your

promotion. She tells you yes, it was clever. Of course she tells you that; it's human nature. She knows you were trying to be clever and that you are hoping for a compliment. So she gives you what sounds like one.

A few more phone calls like that make you think that your clever little promotion is a good idea. (Psychologists call this the false consensus effect; we imagine that people agree with us even though they do not.)

But the basic message of this—"Use us, we're clever"—can make you look silly.

It also can make it seem that because you have nothing important to say, you tell lame jokes instead.

If you think your promotional idea might seem silly or unprofessional, it is.

Being Great vs. Being Good

People in professional services are especially prone to thinking that the better they get, the better their business will be. The more the tax lawyer knows about the tax code, the actuary knows about qualified plans, and the psychologist knows about bipolar personality disorders, the more business will beat a path to their doors.

Two examples suggest this simply is not true, and a third seems to prove it.

The first is on display in every American courtroom today. Brilliant lawyers with a thorough grasp of the law drone on as judges watch the clocks and jurors nod. The lawyers are trying to sell their technical excellence, but their audience—the people who decide whether the lawyer will win or lose—want something else.

The practice of medicine suggests a similar problem. In a remarkably short time, medical science has found cures for the plagues that killed millions of our ancestors: polio, tuberculosis, and smallpox. A woman with a fatally defective heart can now buy a new one. Psychiatrists can now medicate patients with severe disorders and make them far more functional than they could be ten years ago. The medical industry clearly has become technically more competent and expert. The industry clearly has become much better at delivering the expert part of its service.

And so the medical industry should be riding a wave of popularity. Yet 37 percent of people say doctors lack a genuine interest in their patients. Less than half believe that doctors explain things well to patients. Doctors believe that technical proficiency is the measure of their worth, but patients view the relationship side as so critical—there's even a name for it, bedside manner—that they think medicine is failing as a service.

But the best evidence that superior performance is not critical to success in services probably comes from the financial markets. In the 1995 Goldman

Sachs report *The Coming Evolution of the Money Management Industry*, the firm confessed that the real business of money management is not skillfully managing money. It is "gathering and retaining assets"—marketing, to cut right to the point. Is Goldman Sachs simply ignoring their clients' insistence on performance? Not at all. When asked to rank the most important criteria for choosing an investment firm, clients consistently put return on investment—the best evidence of technical proficiency in investing—*below* trust and other "relationship issues." In one survey, clients rated track record ninth out of seventeen attributes, rating it below "a sincere desire for a long-term relationship," among other seemingly soft criteria.

Prospects do not buy how good you are at what you do. They buy how good you are _at who you are._

Superiority

David Ogilvy, who turned his genius for advertising into the famous Ogilvy & Mather agency and, later, a huge chateau in France, once observed that marketers are wrong to emphasize superiority.

Ogilvy argued you can accomplish just as much by convincing a prospect that your service is "positively good."

You can test the validity of Ogilvy's observation with your own experience:

How often are you really looking for the very best service: the very best baby-sitter, cleaning lady, or tax adviser? (Not often.)

How often do you even know the best when you find it? (Not often.)

How long are you willing to look to find the very best, when someone very good is readily available? (Not long.)

How much more will you pay for the very best, especially if very good is good enough? (Not much.)

How much do you trust other people's assessment of the "very best"? (Not much.)

How good does anything have to be to satisfy you? (Only very good; anything better is a bonus.)

And a critical question: How do you respond when a service tells you it is the very best? (Skeptically, and not very well; it sounds like bragging and puffing.)

People who conduct oral surveys for service clients quickly learn something surprising and disappointing to their clients. If the surveyor asks: "What is the main reason you continue to do business with this company?" the most common answer they hear, even from clients of superior services, is "I just feel *comfortable* with them."

Not superiority. Not even excellence.

Just simple old leather-slippers comfort.

Our competitive culture fills us with the desire to be Number One. It's exciting to be part of the best;

best *does* have its rewards. But the assumption that being the very best is a necessary marketing position, much less a uniquely powerful one, is refuted by experience: your own.

Convey that you are "positively good."

The Clout of Reverse Hype

A gutsy professional firm once demonstrated the weakness of hype by creating a truly unusual ad.

Their little ad understated everything. They eliminated almost every adjective. Out went "unique" along with its modest replacement, "distinctive." They slashed "exceptional," too—except the exceptional that referred to the quality of many competitive firms!

And so it went.

The resulting ad's impact was—even in the words of these professionals who despised hyperbole—"remarkable."

For days, professional peers stopped the firm's members on the street to remark on the ad. Despite the firm's relatively tiny size, it received dozens of inquiries from prospective hires who before then had never heard of the firm. Executives from noncompeting firms called the office manager to ask who had created the ad. Other executives contacted the creators to ask for an ad just like it—"something everyone will notice and talk about."

People notice marketing communications that refuse to strain the truth because people notice the unusual, and understatement is unusual.

Far better to say too little than too much.

The First Banks Lesson: People Hear What They See

A researcher once asked twenty business owners what several First Banks' commercials were communicating—and shocked the creators.

These commercials featured an attorney preparing to climb Everest. His preparation included studying previous climbs, weather patterns, and other pertinent information. The Banks' explicit message, intoned by the announcer, was that success in anything requires information, and that First Banks had "the information you need to make good financial decisions."

But the people watching the commercial didn't hear the words. They saw the pictures, most of which showed the attorney practicing rock climbing. From those pictures, those people decided that First Banks was saying it was strong and solid, like the man and mountain, apparently—a message totally unintended by the people who created the commercial.

People hear what they see. A memorable 1980 ad for an interior decorator in Portland, Oregon, suggested it:

"The longer your office says 'Struggling Young Attorney,'" the headline read, "the longer the struggle."

People cannot see your service. So, as the ad reminds us, they judge your service by what they can see. If people see one thing while you are saying another, the First Banks example shows that seeing really is believing: *People will trust their eyes far before they will ever trust your words.*

Look at your business card. Your lobby. Your shoes. What do your visibles say about the invisible thing you are trying to sell?

Watch what you show.

Make the Invisible Visible

We hear someone say, "He bought it sight unseen."

They say it—and we hear it—with amazement. We cannot imagine someone buying something without seeing it first.

Potential buyers are hesitant to consider things they cannot see. So they emphasize what they *can* see.

As a result, visual symbols of a service become important. Willy Loman, in Arthur Miller's *Death of a Salesman*, knew the importance of a shoeshine because he knew that people look for clues. Lawyers devote intense attention to having the right end tables, chairs, and lighting that will capture their essence. Most accountants dress carefully and conservatively by conscious design, to communicate that they are methodical and attentive to detail.

Consciously or subconsciously, these people are performing an act of marketing. They are trying to make the invisible visible.

Not surprisingly, the industry that best understands the importance of visualizing the invisible offers the least visible service of all: insurance. Prudential has its Rock of Gibraltar, Travelers its umbrella, Allstate its Good Hands, Transamerica its tower, Wausau its railroad station. Each uses a visual metaphor to describe the company.

Many services, recognizing this principle and the principle that services are simply relationships among people, visualize their business with the person behind it: Charles Schwab, Henry Block, Colonel Sanders, Dave Thomas, Joel Hyatt, and Wolfgang Puck.

Ad agencies have constantly visualized their service through their people: through Leo Burnett (Leo Burnett), David Ogilvy (Ogilvy & Mather), Jay Chiat (Chiat Day), Bill Bernbach (Doyle Dane Bernbach), and Mary Wells (Wells, Rich & Green).

Consider, too, the leather portfolios that investment firms use to symbolize prosperity, the Doric columns that many law firms use to symbolize longevity, or the padded shoulders that the armed services use to symbolize strength.

Prospects look for visual clues about a service. If they find none, they often look to services that do have them. So provide clues.

Make sure people <u>see</u> who you are.

The Orange Test

You go to a store looking for oranges. You sort through the batch; choose the richest, orangest ones; and take them home.

You have been fooled.

There is no correlation between the orangeness of an orange and its flavor. Growers pick oranges when they are green, and at that moment, the oranges are as rich, ripe, and juicy as they will ever be.

The rich orange color is actually the orange growers' trick. The growers take the green oranges into the plant and "gas" them with an ethylene compound, which breaks down the chlorophyll in the peel that makes the peel green. (In states where it is still legal, growers also may dye the orange with Red Dye Number 2). So the orangeness is not an assurance of flavor. It is the result of all the extra chemicals and labor that went into fooling us, and for which we pay extra every time we buy an orange.

Yet even people who know this still pluck out the orangest oranges from the grocery's stock. People who know better—*people like me*—still are fooled by the orange's package.

This sounds very familiar, because every day in every city and town, this same act plays itself out when people choose a service. Not knowing what's really inside the service, people look to the outside. Unable to see the service, they choose it based solely on the things they can see—in many cases, *even when they know better.*

Seeing is believing. So check your peel.

Our Eyes Have It: The Lessons of Chicago's Restaurants

Richard Melman is the wizard behind Scoozi's, Ed Debevic's, and several of Chicago's other most popular restaurants.

Many connoisseurs take Melman's success as another sign that image is everything, that in restaurants, looking good is better than cooking good.

The critics miss the point. They assume that restaurants are in the food business. Not so; *restaurants are in the entertainment business.* People go to restaurants for the *experience.* They even go to famous restaurants with great cuisine—like the Mansion at Turtle Creek or 510 Groveland—to see what all the fuss is about, to experience what others have, to see who might be there, and to dress up.

Melman's success, then, illustrates the wisdom of knowing what business you are really in, and selling what people are buying.

But Melman's critics also ignore another factor in

Melman's success that is important to any marketer. Few people have discriminating tastes like the late James Beard, who could discern the entire recipe for a complex sauce from one sip. Instead, our perceptions of the quality of almost everything—from professional advice to veal scallopini—are often unsophisticated. Because of this, our perceptions are very vulnerable to influence. When we try the roast duck at the Mansion at Turtle Creek, for example, it tastes good in large part because of the glowing reviews, the gorgeous atmosphere, and the stratospheric prices. Can most of us really taste the difference in the Mansion's roast duck? Not at all.

Like good restaurateurs, service marketers must create the visual surroundings—from the parking lot to the last page of the proposal—that will enhance the client's perception of quality. Offer quality without creating that perception of quality and you have failed the client, and yourself.

Everything visual associated with your service sends a powerful clue about your service. The influence of these visual clues is not superficial; they go to the very heart of your "product" and your relationship with the client.

Watch—and perfect—the visual clues you send.

How to Save
Half a Million

You can walk into several large local service companies and find almost $500,000 worth of sales brochures displayed on their walls.

What you cannot do is tell where those brochures came from and what company stands behind them.

No two look the same. No two reinforce a common message.

Their inconsistency makes the company look inconsistent and disorganized. A whole set of negative associations follow from that.

If you run Bob's Business Services, you want people to say "Oh, that brochure is from Bob's Business Services." Words alone will not get that response because our memories are primarily visual. We remember faces but forget names. So show a common face. Make that investment worthwhile.

Repeat yourself visually, too. It makes you look more organized and professional, and easier to remember.

The Hearsay Rule

Thanks to O.J. Simpson's "Trial of the Century," millions more people now know something about the hearsay rule.

The Hearsay Rule puzzles many viewers and law students, but rests on a basic human principle: To evaluate what someone says, a person needs to see the speaker. The jurors must see the witness; they cannot just hear what the witness says.

This principle of presenting a legal argument also applies to presenting the argument for a service. Prospects need to see you to decide about you. They want to see signals that convey who you are—even the subtlest signals: Your watch—is it showy? Your shoes—are the backs polished, too? Your eyes—do they suggest you are not telling the whole truth?

The prospect is being invited into a relationship, and wonders—*with whom?*

Who are these people?

This is what the prospect is asking, yet most service companies ignore the question. They institutionalize their company instead of personalizing it. The prospect wants to see flesh and blood; the company shows brick and mortar—a picture of the building and some symbols for the service. Or the company shows stock photos of paid models shaking hands or meeting to discuss an important issue in this company, where none of them work.

Good salespeople know better. They know that if

a prospect declines a face-to-face meeting but requests "some information about your company," they rarely will make the sale. They know the prospect must see them to believe them, and buy.

The salesperson knows this principle of selling a service, which is the principle behind the Hearsay Rule: People must see who is saying something to decide whether they will buy it.

Give your marketing a human face.

Metaphorically Speaking: The Black Hole Phenomenon

For years, physicists discussed an important phenomenon: the gravitationally completely collapsed object.

Physicists knew these objects had profound implications. These objects could answer the question "How did the universe begin, and how might it end?"

For years, this discussion was just among leading physicists. Then some creative physicist devised a better name for a gravitationally completely collapsed object.

He called it a black hole.

Suddenly, the whole world was interested. People were intrigued by the concept of a hole in space, which itself already seemed like an enormous hole.

The idea of something black in space, which already is black—well, this whole concept intrigued millions of people.

Now people were talking. Sci-fi movies featured half-mad cowboy astronauts rushing suicidally into black holes.

The words "black hole" changed how people thought. Most important, the words helped people get the idea of a gravitationally completely collapsed object.

Your words matter. One word or metaphor can quickly define your concept and your uniqueness, and make your concept compelling.

If you are selling something complex, simplify it with a metaphor.

The Generative Power of Words: The Gettysburg Address

The battlefield was not a testament to heroism. It was an ugly health hazard—a field of corpses that deeply concerned Pennsylvania's governor.

Nor was that corpse-strewn field a monument to greatness. The North's general, Meade, had so bungled the battle, leaving Lee to regroup, that he submitted his resignation to President Lincoln. But Meade's opponent, Lee, had done no better, marching blindly into slaughter—a blunder so great that he submitted his resignation, too.

The battlefield was Gettysburg, and no one— aside from the people who teach American history or those who have read Garry Wills's *Lincoln at Gettysburg*—sees Gettysburg as it was. Instead, they see Gettysburg as a symbol of heroism and a testament to people's commitment to their beliefs.

The enormous gulf between the perception of Gettysburg and the reality can be explained in 276 words: the Gettysburg Address. With one deft speech, Lincoln changed almost everything—including our view of the Declaration of Independence and the view of millions of Americans living then and now.

Lincoln's address vividly demonstrates the generative power of words: the power of words not simply to describe reality, but to create it. Our perception of Gettysburg has become the reality, just as our perceptions are changed by words every day.

With six ingenious words—"We're Number Two, we try harder"—Avis changed reality in the car rental business. With "when it absolutely positively has to be there overnight," Federal Express swallowed up an enormous share of the overnight delivery business. With "the personal computer," Apple Computer got computers into homes and accelerated a revolution in civilization. Later, with two words, "desktop publishing," Apple created a concept that made the purchase of that "home" computer not merely tolerable to corporations, but desirable.

Some words are wisps; others are warheads. The famous direct-mail writer John Caples once changed one word in an ad—substituting "fix" for "repair"—and increased the response to the ad 20 percent.

In the invisible world of services, where precious little can be shown and everything must be described, words are the ultimate weapons. Hollow and lazy words generate hollow and lazy responses—if any. Active, fresh, powerful words can do more than merely describe reality. Like Lincoln's words, words can change, shape, and even create reality.

Remember Gettysburg, and the generative power of words.

A Robe Is Not a Robe

Decades ago, Macy's department store was sitting on a pile of terrycloth robes.

They were nice robes.

Then a genius named Bernice Fitzgibbon grabbed them.

"They aren't robes anymore," she said. "They're *blotters*. That's what the Europeans call them. That's how I'll sell them."

Fitzgibbon's ads for Blotters started a run on Macy's inventory. Sales skyrocketed.

Macy's terrycloth robe was still just a terrycloth robe.

Or was it?

Sometimes, it's all in how you say it.

Balderdash

Of course you are "committed to excellence."

Of course you have "a tradition of quality service."

Of course you are "responsive."

And of course, you have become—in nineties-speak—"proactive" and "cost-effective."

But really: When a company pitches *you* that story, do you even try to catch it? Do you listen? Do you trust them?

No, No, No?

You don't listen to clichés. Your clients won't either.

Improve the Silence

Let's pick on accounting firms. They're the worst offenders.

Call an accounting firm and request a brochure.

When the brochure arrives, try to read it. Try to figure out quickly what makes that firm an excellent choice.

You can't. And by the way, you won't try.

You'll read the first three paragraphs, then quit. You know it's vague generalizations, not concrete examples. Puff. No proof, no evidence, no interest. Just words—especially adjectives.

Communications like these tell your prospects one thing:

They say *you are willing to waste that person's time*. No message can hurt you more.

Every prospect hopes you will heed the old New England proverb: "Don't talk unless you can improve the silence."

Get to the point or you will never get to the close.

What's Your Point?

Bob Boylan of Successful Presentations in Minneapolis has built a useful book and a solid business around a presentation concept distilled into three words: What's Your Point?

It's based on Bob's discovery that most presenters don't really know what their point is.

Usually, their point is "I want to sell you something." But to the listener, that point is obvious and meaningless.

Most marketing communications fail for the same reason. They never tell you what their point is.

Tell people—in a single compelling sentence— why they should buy from you instead of someone else.

The Vividness Effect

Just as prospects put great value in *recent* information in making their buying decisions, they also are strongly influenced by *vivid* information. Vivid experiences can take over huge parts of a prospect's memory.

No great salesman better illustrated this Vividness Effect than Ross Perot in the 1992 presidential campaign. To sell Perot to people, Perot used two primary weapons: vivid metaphors (three years later, people still remember "silent sucking sound") and vivid pictures (his famous assortment of colorful charts and graphs).

Long after they had forgotten the many dry details

of the debates, people remembered Perot's vivid metaphors and charts. And so, despite his opponents' enormous head start in familiarity, Perot became a formidable competitor—using the vividness effect as his primary marketing weapon.

Perot's weapons were imaginative, but you need not be as spectacular to be vivid. Clear Lake Press in Waseca, Minnesota, recently created a vivid example of its exceptional service. A magazine client needed to print a subscription card to match its other printed materials. Clear Lake's president found an ink company that made a perfect ink match in one try (the client previously had tried twelve matches without luck). The ink company's district manager personally drove the test sample down from Minneapolis to Waseca and then drove it back—almost two hundred miles round-trip.

Fred Betlach of Betlach Jeweler's in Minneapolis uses the vividness effect in the true story of a diamond ring he created for another local jeweler. According to this story, captured in Betlach's brochure, Betlach's finished ring moved the recipient so deeply that she was still crying and unable to talk several hours after she first saw it.

(As further proof that vivid experiences become imprinted in people's memories, people to whom I mention Fred Betlach still ask me, "Is he the jeweler who made that woman cry?")

You can find many ways to be vivid. And you should.

In your words and pictures, make yourself vivid.

Vivid Words

For years, writing teachers have hounded their students to avoid clichés, and to find fresh ways to make their points instead.

It's good marketing advice, too.

People respond to the new and novel and ignore the old, a characteristic that some anthropologists say is a human survival trait. Whenever something new entered a primitive person's environment, he had to study it to decide if it represented a risk. Whatever the explanation, people do respond to things that are new. That is why the very old word "new" still works in advertising.

Sentences free of clichés and other tired words arouse and keep people's curiosity and attention. And fresh words sound sincere, like the real thoughts of the speaker rather than the meaningless recitation of something the speaker read or heard somewhere else, many times before.

Tired clichés and worn-out words bore people. As David Ogilvy once said:

"You cannot bore someone into buying your product."

The Value of Publicity

There are six peaks in Europe higher than the Matterhorn.

Name one.

Get ink.

Advertising Is Publicity

Just when the first snows came to Minnesota in 1994—about the time of the fifth game of the World Series, as luck would have it—a prospect called me. He was desperate to work with me because of the mountain of publicity I had generated for another company in his industry.

I was flattered. But while I did not want to correct the caller, he was wrong. Yes, I had helped generate some publicity for the company—a full-page trade magazine feature, a three-paragraph blurb in a local newspaper business section, and a three-paragraph mention in a national magazine. That was what the company aimed for, and we achieved our objectives. But it was not an avalanche.

Why, then, did it seem like an avalanche to this prospect?

Because we also ran two large ads in that same

trade publication at the same time. In his vague memory, this prospect could not distinguish the ads from the articles. All he remembered was what seemed like a lot of publicity—and he wanted an avalanche, too.

The prospect demonstrated another principle of marketing: Advertising is publicity. Advertising is mention in the public forum from which people learn about and come to know the companies mentioned in the ads.

If you want publicity, advertise.

Advertising Begets Publicity

A public relations person contacted a local business magazine editor with a classic story—the story similar to the dreams of several million American executives trapped right now in downtown office towers.

The story was of a longtime American resident who loved his native Greece and decided to lead some friends on a tour there. The friends raved. This made the man wonder: Could he make a living doing just this?

After weeks of wondering and months of trial and error, he started the business. Years later, that business—the Greek travel agency Hellenic Adventures—is growing rapidly.

But when the public relations person pitched this

classic story, which proves a mother's advice—"Do what you love; the money will follow"—the editor balked again and again. Why?

The problem wasn't that the story had no appeal. It was that the story was just a story to the editor, because he had never heard of Hellenic Adventures. How could he be sure the company was real and viable, his trust in me notwithstanding?

"I'm not sure I can believe in that company," he said to himself. "I've never heard of them."

What would have simplified the public relations person's job? Advertising. If that editor had seen Hellenic Adventures's ads (the company had not yet started frequent advertising) he would have said, "This is a real business, so this is a real story."

Advertising, in short, would have led to publicity.

The elements of a marketing effort are not separate elements. They work together, often in surprising ways. Advertising is publicity; direct mail is advertising; everything mingles and commingles, and virtually everything, done properly, will contribute.

If you want more publicity, do more advertising.

The Essence of Publicity

At this writing, no magazine or newspaper suffers from being too interesting.

In a world deluged with communications, the task of creating an interesting weekly or monthly publication is daunting. With violent speed, editors are brought in and hurled out as increasingly strapped publications search for the formula.

Whatever the formula may be, there is one thing it is not. No publication will get anywhere by running business advertisements thinly disguised as articles.

Your typical press release, cleverly designed to get advertising without paying for it, will not work. In fact, the editors, who know their publication could use the advertising, will resent your effort. Transparent press releases also make their authors look naive and manipulative—an impression no one should make on any editor. The world is too small.

What editors *do* want is to make their publications interesting. They want their readers to say "Loved the article!"

So in efforts to publicize your service, never ask "What makes our service so good?" Instead, ask "What makes our service interesting to that publication's readers?"

If you want editors to help you, help them. Give them something interesting. Give them a story.

Inspiration from William F. Buckley

So all you need to do to generate a little publicity is to be a little interesting.

Great.

So you look around for a little while. And a little while longer. And longer. The next day, you sigh, "I'm not sure there is anything interesting about our company."

Look harder.

John McPhee wrote a fascinating book about oranges. (That's right: *oranges.*)

The TV journalist Harry Reasoner once narrated an enchanting minidocumentary about doors.

Robert Pirsig wrote a best-seller on motorcycle maintenance. Hundreds of thousands of people who never rode a motorcycle read it avidly.

There is no such thing as an uninteresting subject, someone once wrote. There is only an uninterested person.

William F. Buckley gave another meaning to this when someone asked him about his interviews on *Firing Line*. "What happens," the person asked Buckley, "when you get a guest who is not interesting?"

"That never happens," Buckley answered. "If you look deeply enough, ninety-nine out of a hundred people are interesting—and the one hundredth person is interesting because he isn't."

Look harder. The interest—and the story—are there.

Focus on Buying, Not Selling

Some marketing experts recommend that in creating a direct mail program, you should devote half your time to creating the reply form.

Most clients are surprised, if not shocked, when they hear this very revealing rule.

The rule is revealing because it suggests that most marketers spend too much effort on the sale—and too little on the "buy."

Think how often you have been virtually sold on something, but chose not to make the purchase because it was too hard to buy. The salesperson offered all sorts of options, for example, or made you worry about the value of extended warranty, or offered more complicated financing packages than you could not intelligently choose among. *The product was too hard to buy.* Now, think of your opposite experiences. Something appealed to you—a little, not necessarily a lot—and the ease with which you could order, pay for, and receive the product ultimately led you to make the purchase.

Good marketing must focus on the buy. How clear is your offer? Can the prospects sample the service, thereby reducing their risk? How clear is the price? How easy is it to buy?

Make your service easy to buy.

The Most Compelling Selling Message

What sells?

The most compelling selling message you can deliver in any medium is not that you have something wonderful to sell.

It is: "I understand what you need."

The selling message "I have" is about you. The message "I understand" is about the only person involved in the sale who really matters: the buyer.

Find out what they want.

Find out what they need.

Find out who they are.

It will take extra time, but it can make the sale.

Don't sell your service. Sell your prospect.

What Blank Eyes Mean

A salesperson has something to sell you. "Blah, blah, blah," you hear.

He continues. Same thing. You hear the melody, but not the lyrics.

Eventually, you graciously thank him and promise you will get back to him.

Which, of course, you don't.

You know why his pitch failed. Because the person did not talk about *you*. His entire pitch was about *him* and what he had, not about you and what you need.

It was all about him. But what you cared about was you.

Do you know why *your* pitches fail, too?

Talk about him, not about you.

Presenting's First Rule: Imitate Dick

For fourteen months, I enjoyed the strange and wonderful experience of working with Dick Wilson.

Everyone should be so lucky.

Dick is a genius at presenting.

To appreciate his genius, let me set the stage: It is the wood-paneled living room in the historic Pillsbury mansion. Top executives from Musicland have come to Carmichael-Lynch Advertising to hear the agency's pitch. Dick, who will lead the creative presentation, is wearing a coat and tie, but still looks like he has just finished mowing the lawn. After the writer and art director have shown their ideas for Musicland's new TV commercials, Dick rises to summarize. His summary should take five minutes.

It takes forty. Dick emotes, rambles, enthuses. He swerves off on tangents from which even the Musicland execs try to rescue him. The clients are lost. Dick may be lost. But—and this is a huge but—we *never* take our eyes off him. It is not because of what Dick says; it is because of what he feels.

Dick *cares*. He believes in what he is saying, and he *cares*—about doing wonderful commercials that will help Musicland sell millions of records. And in an industry known for slickness, Dick is just Dick. Nothing is planned—how could such a presentation be planned? No clever references to tidbits he has learned about each Musicland executive. No fascinating creative-type tie, no affectations, no attitude—nothing the client might have expected from an award-winning creative director.

Dick won this and four other major presentations in succession, the best winning record in Twin Cities advertising, for four reasons.

He shattered the stereotype.

He never pretended.

He risked showing his true self.

And he cared passionately—and showed clients how much he cared.

You should have seen him.

You should copy him.

Mission Statements

Like movies, books, TV shows, and everything else, there are many bad mission statements. This does not mean that mission statements are inherently bad or that drafting one is foolish. A good one has value, if only to show employees the pot of gold at the rainbow's end.

But mission statements do not belong in your marketing communications. Mission statements tell people where you are going—your strategic goal— and good companies, like good generals, never alert their competitors to where they are going. What's more, a good mission statement describes the future, not the present—and prospects want to know who you are *right now.*

Write a mission statement, but keep it private.

What a Mission Statement Must Be—and Must Have

Make your mission statement specific. Tell employees and stakeholders exactly where to go. If you say, "We're going to San Francisco," people know where to head and can chart their progress. If you say, "We're going west," people may think they've achieved the goal three miles after they start.

Employees want those directions. Nothing confuses employees more and inspires them less than vague marching orders and no road map.

So follow every mission statement with a concrete statement of measurable objectives. Give people a clear target so they can see how achieving those immediate objectives will help them achieve the mission.

Draw a clear map. And after every mission statement, add an objectives statement.

When to Can a Mission Statement

The test of a mission statement is simple. A mission statement must cause change; it must change how people in your company act.

Three weeks after you reveal your mission statement to everyone, ask five employees: Have you done anything differently in the last three weeks because of what the mission statement says?

And are you likely to change anything that you do in the next three weeks?

If you get ten no's, throw out your mission statement.

If your mission statement isn't producing, fire it.

What Really Sells

In the factories we make perfume," Revlon founder Charles Revson once said. "But in the stores we sell hope."

So do we all. Everywhere, people are buying happiness, or the hope of it.

Happiness is so important in our country that its pursuit is considered an inalienable right—together with the right to life itself—in our Declaration of Independence.

People want to smile. And will pay handsomely for it.

Sit in on a group of magazine editors reviewing the best-selling covers of the year. The best-sellers are almost always happier and more hopeful.

Sit in on a review of a test of different direct mail letters for the same service. The most upbeat letter almost always wins. (This is why one noted direct mail copywriter advises writers, "Never write when you are worried.")

My wife once recommended a typically sad Swedish film to a co-worker. Her co-worker said, "Forget it. If I want to be unhappy, I can just open my checkbook."

Samsonite once created a brilliant, award-winning ad showing its luggage being dropped out of an airplane. The luggage survived the fall, an incredible reminder of its durability. Unfortunately, the commercial also reminded people of airplane crashes. Sales actually dropped, too.

Bumper stickers now urge people to commit random acts of kindness. Make people smile, the stickers urge.

We want to smile more.

Read through everything you send to clients and prospects.

How does it *feel*?

Does it sell happiness, or the hope of it?

Above all, sell hope.

HOLDING ON TO WHAT YOU'VE GOT: NURTURING AND KEEPING CLIENTS

Relationship Accounting

Huge Account Shifts Agencies," reads the monthly headline in *Advertising Age*, and in the second paragraph you often find a revealing quote.

The jilted agency president says he is "shocked." "We were doing excellent work at Smith & Smith. The client told us she was happy. This is a total surprise."

The president's surprise is genuine—and so is his problem.

His problem is rooted in the nature of service relationships. Unless a service provider like Smith & Smith pays careful attention, it always operates at a deficit. Without knowing it, service providers *always* owe their clients.

This debt dates from the first day, when Smith & Smith wins the account. "Winning" implies that Smith & Smith's people feel they have earned the business. But as Theodore Levitt has convincingly argued, the client sees it differently. Smith & Smith has not earned the business; it merely has earned the *right* to earn the business. The client has assumed all the risk, and from that, feels it has done Smith & Smith a favor. The client has bought something that the agency has not yet delivered. When that something comes, it could be awful, too expensive, or both.

So Smith & Smith already is operating at a deficit. It owes the client one.

Then Smith & Smith begins delivering services: a

storyboard for a TV spot, for example, along with a bill. The client is not sure what it has received or how good it is—just as accountant's and lawyer's clients do not know if they have received a good "product" for a fair price. The client only knows that it owes a lot for something of uncertain value that has not yet produced a return. The deficit now is two.

Smith & Smith soon increases its deficit again. People make mistakes, and Jim at Smith & Smith makes one: He fails to call the client back as promptly as the receptionist promised. Whoever made the mistake—Jim, Jim's receptionist, or the client, by mishearing—Smith & Smith's deficit reaches three.

Now and then, Smith & Smith's president makes a gesture to the client. He sends Godiva chocolates at Christmas, for example. But the president cannot easily overcome the large deficit, because those inevitable mistakes happen faster than the president can mail chocolates. Most clients will overlook these mistakes if Smith and Smith has a surplus in its relationship account. But like most service providers, Smith & Smith has a deficit. So the mistakes go in the debit column.

No one at Smith & Smith realizes how far they are in debt. Service providers always are the last to know, in part because few people like conflict. So clients often bury grievances rather than air them. Service providers think that the silence is golden; they think the lack of complaints means the relationship is going well. But it is growing worse.

This relationship deficit exists in the parties' other significant relationships: their marriages. In both relationships, debts grow without either side knowing. Then one day a frustrated spouse or a frustrated client announces he has had enough. The other spouse and the Smith & Smith president are shocked. Neither person understands the unique accounting in relationships.

Watch your relationship balance sheet; assume it is worse than it appears, and fix it.

The Day After—Why Getting the Business Can Be the First Step in Losing It

You can generate significant sales for a service simply by promising miracles.

After doing that, you have a new client who can't wait for the magic you promised. In short, you have the Client from Hell.

Even if you do a very good job, you have a disappointed client. Your client wasn't expecting a very good job; she was expecting a *great* job. You *promised*.

This phenomenon is the bane of the collections agency industry, and explains why that industry is all churn, a constant business of getting new clients to replace those who are fleeing. The salespeople deliver passionate sales pitches, the clients sign up, the salespeople pocket their commissions, and the client thinks those blankety-blank deadbeats will finally pay.

But those blankety-blanks still don't pay. Only about 21 percent do pay.

Do collections agency prospects ever hear that even a good agency will collect less than 30 percent of the debts outstanding? No. So 79 percent of their prospects end up disappointed, and leave for another agency.

If you make a client think you will do better than you can do, the client will end up disappointed. Even worse, she will decide that you misled her, or lied.

It isn't worth getting that business. A disappointed person who thinks you are a liar will usually tell three other people. Suddenly, one great sale has become four big problems.

Don't raise expectations you cannot meet.

Expectations, Satisfaction, and the Perils of Hype

What dissatisfies a client?

It is not bad service in some absolute sense of "bad." You send a letter to New York that takes three days. Is that bad delivery? Well, it is terrible delivery for an overnight service and hideous delivery for a fax, but it is acceptable delivery for a letter. It is the level of service you have learned to expect. So you are satisfied.

A customer's satisfaction is the gap between what the customer expects and what she gets. Service below her expectations makes her dissatisfied—and the greater the gap, the greater her dissatisfaction.

This means that one of a marketer's most suicidal marketing weapons is hype. Few marketers can resist using hyperbole to boost sales. But does it work for the long term?

Ask IBM. In 1983 IBM introduced its PC Jr. with an uncharacteristic flood of hype. Americans got "Charlie Chaplined" into believing that this new PC would be the IBM of personal computers.

That raised people's expectations enough. The added hot air from what was typically such a modest company inflated expectations even more.

The PC Jr. could never meet those expectations. People who tried the PC Jr. were dissatisfied, because it fell below the enormous expectations that IBM's hype had created.

Because of that debacle, IBM lost a chunk of its customer franchise. If IBM had tried to follow the PC Jr. with a product that really was revolutionary, few would have believed it; IBM had lost the credibility needed to make that claim. It was seven years before IBM earned its way back in, and then only with an exceptional product: the PS 1.

It could just as easily happen to you.

To manage satisfaction, you must carefully manage your customer's expectations.

Your Patrons Are Saints

She has come to you.

She has paid for expensive entrées, your favorite CDs, and part of your kids' upcoming college tuitions.

She has tolerated your mistakes (more than you know).

She has risked her money, her reputation, her peace of mind, and most of her neck. She may even have risked her entire business.

She has smiled through the worst, laughed through the best, and said nice things about you to other people.

And so now you ask, should I call her?

Should I feel any debt?

Should I care about her?

Should I bother to tell her? And if I do tell her, how often should I tell her?

There is no such thing as too often, too grateful, too warm, or too appreciative.

After all she has been through—*more than you know*—you cannot thank your client too much.

And you probably are not doing it enough.

Your parents were right. Say thank you. Often.

Thanks

We tell someone we cannot thank them enough.

We're right; we can't.

Keep thanking.

Few things feel more gratifying than gratitude—and few services express their gratitude as much as they should.

How many notes of thanks did you send last year? A suggestion: Send twice as many this year.

Keep thanking.

Where Have You Gone, Emily Post?

We all get too little thanks, and we yearn for more. The rarer thanks become—and they do seem rarer—the more we value the thanks we get.

A huge national charity asks a working mother to canvas her block to raise funds. Carrying her six-month-old son as she walks, she raises $160— 60 percent more than last year's captain. In return for those three evenings and her own $30 contribution, she never hears from the charity again.

Three weeks later a professional association invites a man to keynote its one-day seminar. He says he can make it only by cutting one day short a vacation to visit his mother and sister. The association begs, and the speaker relents.

Returning from his West Coast vacation, the speaker gets stranded in Denver. He arrives in Minneapolis just in time to fuzzbust his way to the conference. He catches his breath and delivers his speech. The audience responds very enthusiastically. The seminar hosts barely respond. They mail a four-sentence form letter to all thirteen speakers.

Five weeks later a famous art institution asks a prominent professional to donate an evening to consult the institute. She does, rushing from dinner to arrive early. A week later she, like her three fellow contributors, receives a two-paragraph form letter. With it is a certificate for 20 percent off any art shop purchase exceeding $50. In short, the institute thanks the woman for her entire evening away from her family and for $425 worth of professional advice by agreeing to make a slightly smaller profit on her next significant purchase.

How would you feel about those services?

Would you contribute to their success? Would you promote and patronize them?

Would you recommend them?

And these experiences also make me wonder:

Did these services know the impression they were making and the harm they were causing?

Have we forgotten to say thank you? Have you forgotten?

Do you thank people enough? Are you sure?

Poised for a Fall

Brace yourself.

A typical service client cannot tell when the service is performed well. He cannot tell if the motivational speaker really motivated his salespeople, if the tailor made the perfect alterations to make the suit most flattering, or if the lawyer won a motion that another lawyer would have lost.

But a typical client is very good at seeing that the speech fell flat, that the pant legs are ¼" too long, and that the court denied his attorney's motion.

In short, few clients know how good they have it—but all of them know how bad.

And so, the central fact of service marketing is this frustrating one: *It is much easier to fail in a service than to succeed.*

To make matters worse, most service relationships are not deeply cultivated: a few meetings here, a couple of lunches there. Add up those hours, and they rarely equal two dates. Unfortunately, trust takes time—more than two dates' worth. And so service failures, which are much more obvious than successes, erode the client's already weak trust at the heart of the relationship.

Given that failures are obvious but most successes are invisible, what must you do?

Advertise your successes. Show your client what you have done.

If you beat the deadline by two days (a good idea), make sure the client knows.

If you came under the estimate by 7 percent (an even better idea), make sure the client knows.

If you are especially proud of something you did, make sure the client knows.

Don't expect the client to see how hard you have worked, how much you have cared, and how well you have performed. So often, the client is the last to know.

Make sure the client knows.

Satisfaction and Services

How do you satisfy a service customer? With surprising difficulty—as you will realize when you compare it to your own experiences with buying products.

You decide to buy a car, for example. Our world

being arranged as it is—around the automobile—you need a car. If you are typical, you also *desire* a car and may even *covet* a particular one: the leather seats, the special trim packages, the six coats of paint, and the messages that car conveys.

When you buy that car, you are satisfied the second you pull out of the dealership. The car is just what you wanted.

After you buy a product, it constantly reinforces your satisfaction. You golf, for example. You covet and buy a Titleist Tour 100 balata golf ball. Each time you wash and wipe off the ball, the white-on-white finish that attracted and satisfied you from the beginning reminds you what a smart purchase you made and how satisfied you are. Each time you strike the ball well, the ball's high arc through the air and soft landing on the distant green reminds you again. Your Tour 100 ball continually satisfies you—just as the car, a flattering sweater, or that big-screen TV satisfies you constantly by its presence. Seeing is believing, and what you see makes you feel satisfied.

Now, the contrast: You decide you might need a service. Your roof leaks or your tooth aches, for example. You rarely desire a particular service, and almost never covet one. In fact, you regard many services as necessary evils—the lawyer you must hire to resolve a dispute, the accountant you must retain because you cannot deal with complicated books, the insurance you must own should disaster strike. In most cases, you are less eager and enthusiastic—and less satisfied—when you choose a service.

Unlike products that you buy, the services you use come, then go. They do not stick around to remind you of your satisfaction and to encourage you to purchase them again. The lawn the neighbor boy mows nicely one day needs mowing again just days later; the tooth the dentist filled no longer aches, but nothing about the filled tooth satisfies you or reminds you of the good service you received. Your much-needed insurance policy is just sitting in a file somewhere, doing nothing at all. You no longer can see the few visible reminders of these services that you received. Your satisfaction with them is primarily a memory.

So the typical service deliverer—like you—is not present to make its clients conscious of the benefits that the service still is providing: the pipes that are now draining properly, the insurance coverage that provides much-needed disability coverage for the sole proprietor, the contract addendum that retains for the author valuable rights for his book. The homeowner with the fixed pipes was satisfied for a couple days, then forgot about it. The business proprietor and the author one day may be very satisfied—but for now, they are not even aware of the service; the question of satisfaction does not even arise.

Given these significant differences between typical product and service buyers and their satisfaction, what should the service marketer do to create a satisfied client?

Stay present. Advertising and publicity reminds clients and former clients of the satisfying service that you once provided, and assures them that you still are around, viable, and successful. Create a feeling of satisfaction by showing the client how you are satisfying others. Communicate your successes: new clients, new successes, new awards, new recognition, new testimonials, growth in staff and revenues.

A product continually reminds its buyers that it is good. With appropriate modesty, you must, too.

Out of sight is out of mind.

QUICK FIXES

Manage the Tiny Things

I recently interviewed three people to subcontract for a client's project.

I already had decided that each person was skilled enough. That's why I called each one.

Choosing the best candidate was easy. I hired the person who wrote back after the interviews first.

So often, and more often than we imagine, that is the difference in a sale. Not superior knowledge. Not superior talent or years of experience. Just something tiny. Like a short thoughtful letter.

Sweat the smallest stuff.

One Ring

Fallon McElligott sells very creative advertising. That means that it sells its creative people. And creative people are difficult. Egos. They'll be done whenever. And so what if it costs lots of money?

That's the stereotype, anyway.

Several summers ago, I decided that my three-on-three basketball team really needed Jamie Barrett, a 6′ 5″ forward/copywriter at Fallon McElligott. So during my recruiting campaign, and later during our season, I often called Jamie at work.

I would reach Fallon's receptionist in one ring, and Jamie one ring and a split second later. It could be the world's fastest phone system. The first three times I tapped into it I wasn't ready to talk. I didn't expect Jamie to answer so suddenly.

Those calls left an amazing impression.

Those three seconds in three different phone calls convinced me that Fallon really delivered service, that Fallon made you feel respected and wanted, which¹ is critical for a service. Those calls told me that Fallon wasn't an undisciplined, arrogant, screw-service-it's-beneath-us bunch after all.

Amazing. Three seconds.

Now I am telling the world. People in a dozen cities will read this and decide that Fallon delivers great service *and* very creative advertising.

Service like that is worth whatever it costs.

Your business starts with the first call. How good is yours?

Speed

Life is lickety-split. Dayton-Hudson Corporation's chairman rallies employees with a line from *Future Shock:* "Speed is Life." Comedian Steven Wright captured the current pace of life when he deadpanned about his microwave fireplace, "You can spend an evening in front of it in only eight minutes."

To many people, the world seems driven out of whack with all this speed. We fax when we could mail. We rush out of habit. It seems we really do want microwave fireplaces.

There is no logic to all this speed.

There also is no point in arguing; speed is where the world is going.

Be fast. Then get faster.

Say P.M., Deliver A.M.

The first time you have something to deliver for a client, try this: Say you'll have it to him at 1 P.M. Then deliver it at 11 A.M.

Do it the next time, too.

Now you have money in the bank. You may need it. And you'll be glad you had it.

Say P.M., deliver A.M.

Note to Myself

Something suddenly struck me. I grabbed a pen and jotted on a yellow Post-it note the first value of my business:

Make every client very happy every day.

Something from a self-help book: corny and obvious.

It almost embarrasses me.

But it does something else: *It works*.

It changes how I talk, how I sound (like I am smiling), what I say, and how well I listen. It reminds me how lucky I am to have this person place so much faith in me.

Now, how do I talk, sound, and listen when the note gets buried under my other papers? Different—honest.

So do something corny. Put that note by your phone.

Shoot the Message, Not the Messenger: The Fastest Way to Improve Your Sales Force

In fifteen seconds, Clifford could talk your children into attending Yale.

Judy could quiet an entire room with her passionate defense of her position on abortion.

Fred has convinced eleven of his friends to buy Shad Rap fishing lures.

Then I ask the brokerage company executive about these three people—her fellow partners. Are they pretty good at selling? "Oh, they're OK." Are they selling effectively now? "Not really. Not nearly as well as we'd like."

What's the problem?

With few exceptions, the problem is not the sales force. Like most people, Clifford, Judy, and Fred are extremely adept at selling things they believe in. This company's selling problem is actually a marketing problem: The company has failed to create or identify the distinction that makes a selling message powerful, and that makes the salespeople true believers.

Sent off to pitch prospects, Clifford, Judy, and Fred start from weakness. Their message sounds fuzzy; they don't sound truly convinced and confident. It's no wonder. The key to any effective presentation is having a clear point of view. If you have one you believe in, you are almost certain to be effective in presenting it.

Does your sales force have that clear point of view? A few people may. But if your firm has not created or clearly identified its distinction, and the benefits of that distinction, to people who use the service, most people will not present your case effectively for one simple reason: *You haven't developed that case.*

To fix your messengers, fix your message.

Personal Investment

Say "risk" to businesspeople, and they hear "money."

Sometimes, they're right. But many of the risks that people fail to take—and the rewards they miss because of it—cost nothing. These risks are *personal*.

Consider the director of an exceptional service. The service is excellent, but the sales are merely good. Why? Because the director refuses to take the personal risks involved in personally selling his product. A big convention of prospects comes to town. Afraid to risk himself among strangers, the director "gets sick" on the day of the convention. On another occasion, someone mentions a good prospect for the director in the same town. The director never calls the prospect.

Gail Sheehy illuminated the rewards of risk-taking in her book *Pathfinders*. Sheehy began her research looking for the secrets of truly contented people. She wondered what made these people feel such a sense of well-being. Sheehy learned that "people of high well-being" shared just a few traits, and this was one:

They all had taken an enormous risk.

Selling a service involves personal risks. You can look too pushy. You can be rejected. (No, you *will* be rejected.) People won't return your calls. You run the risk of feeling bad when you go home at night.

But the rewards of all those efforts will make you wonder: Why didn't I do that in the first place?

Taking risks doesn't always mean risking your money. Sometimes, it just means risking *yourself.*

Risk yourself.

The Collision Principle

Kurt Vonnegutt, Jr.'s *God Bless You, Mr. Rosewater* contains some excellent advice for every marketer.

Mr. Rosewater, Sr., recognizing that his son, Eliot, had neither the brains nor the talent to become hugely successful, gave Eliot the best advice under the circumstances:

"Eliot, someday a large sum of money will change hands. Make sure you are in the middle of it."

Mr. Rosewater's advice inspired me when a gifted graphic designer asked my advice on her new career.

I said, "Just get out there. Get in opportunity's way. Let it hit you."

It applies to every service marketer. For all the talk about improving service quality, positioning, research, targeted direct mail—for all the art and science of marketing—much of growing a business is where you happen to sit on a flight to New York one afternoon.

People don't want to spend days making decisions. They have little time, and books like *Overworked American* suggest that they have less time every year. People meet you, they like you, pretty soon they hire you. Some people propose on their first date, after all. Many people in business move even faster.

Get out there. Almost anywhere. Let opportunity hit you.

SUMMING UP

You outline a business problem to a group.

Finance says it's a resource problem.

Human Resources says it's a people problem.

Research says it's an information problem.

And Marketing says there's no problem—just double the marketing budget.

But more and better marketing is not the answer to every business question. For all its marketing brilliance, for example, McDonald's probably would have fallen into bankruptcy without its brilliant real estate strategy—the strategy that today accounts for most of the company's revenues and $8.8 *billion* of its book value. For all the brilliant campaigns that established its brand in overnight delivery, Federal Express never would have flown without Fred Smith's skillful negotiating and lobbying in Washington. And without the company's mastery of systems and logistics, Federal Express's clever campaigns probably would have killed the company. Millions of people attracted by the ads would have discovered that the service absolutely positively did not work. They would have told their friends, and that would have destroyed the company's reputation.

To succeed spectacularly in a service business, you must get all your ducks in a row. Marketing is just one duck.

But it is one *very* big duck. Take the case of American Express: In 1972, you could herd American

Express's entire marketing department into a bus shelter—just fifteen people with a budget of $4 million. Today, few people can count all the employees in the department, and the ad budget alone exceeds $210 million.

And that money has been very well spent. Ogilvy & Mather's "Do you know me?" and "Don't leave home without it" campaigns brilliantly focused and communicated the company's position and status and propelled the company to a place that ordinary merchandising *never* would have taken it.

This book also devotes fifteen pages to the importance of service brands. Five years ago, this book would not have mentioned them, because I was deeply influenced by all the rumors about the decline of brands. Then I watched dozens of branded services beat superior services, for no apparent reason other than their brand.

We hear so much about service quality today. But much of service quality is simply—here's that word again—*invisible* to the client. And for marketing purposes—for the purpose of attracting and keeping business—a service is only what prospects and clients perceive it to be. So "get better reality": Improve your service quality. But never forget that the prospect and client must perceive that quality.

When we are clients of a hotel, for example, we know our room has been spotlessly cleaned. We do not hold that perception because the room actually *is* spotless. We believe that the room is spotless because, as Theodore Levitt perceptively has pointed out, the hotel has wrapped each glass tightly in paper and covered the toilet seat with a sanitized wrap. We do not see the quality; we see these symbols of quality that say "clean room." It is not the hotel's service quality that wins us; it is the hotel's *merchandising* of its quality.

Our methods for choosing a service are often wild and seemingly arbitrary—anything but intelligent, cost-benefit–oriented behavior. This suggests that you cannot expect to seize a market just by creating a provably superior service with a demonstrably higher benefit-to-cost ratio. The success of American Express suggests something much different.

Services are human. Their successes depend on the relationships of people. People are human—frustrating, unpredictable, temperamental, often irrational, and occasionally half mad. But you can spot some patterns in people. The more you can see the patterns and better understand people, the more you will succeed—and this book was written with the hope that it will help you do just that.

Recommended Reading for Service Marketers

Because many of marketing's greatest battles are not waged in the market, but in the minds of prospects, understanding how people think helps you understand how to market and sell.

You see that emphasis throughout this book.

My interest in thinking was inspired by watching people in two different companies stumble through marketing planning. The thinking I saw proved that synergy is a myth: Two heads may be better than one, but twelve heads are worse.

I then read Peter Senge's *The Fifth Discipline* to help me understand systems thinking. I recommend the book, even though it is tough wading. I also recommend Ichak Adizes's *Corporate Life Cycles*. It can help you understand how people tend to think at different stages of a company's life.

There are thousands of books on the human mind and memory, but even my strong performance in Psychology 101 does not qualify me to choose among them. I benefited from *Decision Traps* by J. Edward Russo and Paul J. H. Schoemaker, *Influence* by Robert Cialdini, and *How We Know What Isn't So* by Thomas Gilovich. None of these books require an advanced degree in psychology, and all three remind me that in so many things in life, "logic has nuthin' to do with it."

For years, I worked with art directors on ads, trusting our intuitions. We thought our intuitions about people were enough; they weren't. And we all misuse the word "intuition." We imply that intuitions are instinctive, perhaps even extrasensory. But my intuitions about O.J. Simpson's guilt or innocence, for example, reflect my previous experiences with alleged wife-batterers, the reliability of legal evidence, and with the man himself—with a large volume of information. My intuitions, like everyone else's, are based on information and experience: They are based on data. The more and better information we have about people, including about how people think and make decisions, the better our intuitions will be.

Away from the psychology section you can find several books about the distinctive requirements for marketing a service. Jan Carlzon introduces *Moments of Truth*, a notion that is similar to my discussion of points of contact. Ronald Zemke's *The Service Edge* lists hundreds of examples of excellent service and strongly recommends listening and surveying. Tom Peters's books are filled with examples and have influenced most people's thoughts about service. Whenever someone thinks of getting "close to the customer," for example, those are Peters's four words vibrating in their head.

Regis McKenna's *The Regis Touch* and Paul Hawken's *Growing a Business* include very good discussions about the importance of relationships in marketing.

In the service marketing section, however, the shelves are almost empty. You will find books with titles like *Marketing Your Services*. Most of them are books for consultants and sole proprietors, however, with advice like "Get published in magazines, give speeches, join the local Chamber of Commerce." This is good advice, to be sure, but people to whom it is new and valuable information probably should not enter business.

Perhaps the most widely distributed book on service marketing is *Marketing Services*, by Leonard Berry and A. Parasuraman. The book's strength is in the first half, which puts the emphasis in service marketing where the emphasis belongs: getting the service right.

On communicating, I recommend Strunk and White's *The Elements of Style* and William Zinsser's *On Writing Well*. I also recommend David Ogilvy's *Confessions of an Advertising Man*, a book so interesting that my mother read it thirty-five years ago just for fun.

But nothing I can recommend will help you create names as ingenious as NameLab, themes as effective as "We're Number Two, we try harder," or concepts as clever as negotiable certificates of deposit. I believe imagination is the greatest possible asset in marketing, in part because imagination is rare and, in all likelihood, unteachable.

On positioning, Ries and Trout's *Positioning* is a classic. A bearable flaw of the book—no book can cover everything—is that the authors stress how the human mind works, yet ignore volumes of research on the influence of recency and vividness on the mind. Ries and Trout suggest that positioning is not heavily dependent on the words and images used. They seem to suggest that good positioning statements make strong headlines and theme lines. Cynics might suggest that Ries and Trout deemphasized words and images and downsized the importance of creativity because their ad agency's creative product was weak. Maybe so. It is wise to read their book—a very good book—with that in mind.

On presenting, I recommend Bob Boylan's *What's Your Point?* and anything by Ron Hoff. Most of all, however, I recommend watching a presentation by my former boss, Dick Wilson. Some things cannot be explained; they must be seen. A Dick Wilson presentation is one of them.

On marketing generally, and service marketing particularly, I save my strongest recommendation for last: Theodore Levitt's *The Marketing Imagination*, particularly chapters 5 and 6. Levitt strongly influenced my sections on relationship deficits and the importance of visibles.

Nothing beats experience, of course, but reading books about others' experiences comes in a competent second. The risk in learning only from personal experience is that too often, we draw conclusions from too little data—we learn too much from too little. We also tend to credit our company's successes to everything that went into them—the classic fallacy *Post hoc ergo prompter hoc* (It happened after the fact; therefore it happened because of that fact). And so we keep repeating things that hurt our business.

In *Decision Traps*, Russo and Schoemaker tell the amusing story of the man who explains how he won the huge Spanish lottery. The man chose a number ending in 48. He said he knew the winning number would end in 48 because for seven days before he picked the number, he woke up thinking of the number seven. "And seven times seven is forty-eight," he said. "So of course, I picked 48!"

All people act like the Spanish lottery winner at times. We mislead ourselves. We link our successes and failures to things that barely influenced the outcome. In marketing, for example, we sometimes decide that a tactic has failed only because we do not see the impact when we expected it. Years later, we often discover that the tactic worked perfectly, just slowly, and even unpredictably.

So my recommendation to anyone marketing in this new economy is to learn all you can from your experiences and from the experiences of others. These books help.

Acknowledgments

"Writing a book is like having a baby," James Simon Kunen wrote in his preface to *The Strawberry Statement*. "Both bring something new into the world, and both are a pain in the ass." Writing this book was like giving birth, but much better than Kunen described: Like my children, this book seems like a miracle.

So, thank you:

My friend Cliff Greene, who unwittingly started this project by imploring me to speak to the strategic planning committee of Temple Israel in Minneapolis.

My friend Sue Crolick, who happened to turn over a long note I had sent her, found the Temple Israel speech on the back (I was saving paper by using both sides), and insisted I get the speech published.

Editor Jay Novak, who, aided by Allison Campbell's skilled editing, printed that revised speech and its sequels in his magazine.

Literary agent Eric Vrooman, who one afternoon came across that article in Jay's magazine, thought it represented the start of a good book, and called to suggest we "put something together." This book would not exist without Eric and his many talents.

Publisher Mel Parker at Warner Books, who agreed the article could make a worthy book, and then made it happen.

Jonathon Lazear, Sarah Nelson Hunter, Susie Moncur, and Dennis Cass at the Lazear Agency, who provided world-class service.

The angels at Warner: Sharon Krassney, whose warmth made me feel at home high over Avenue of the Americas, and Jimmy Franco and Jeffrey Theis, who spread the word.

My great teachers: Harriet Evenson, Errol Duke, James Robinson, Jens Robinson, Ron Rebholz, David Kennedy, William Clebsch, David Potter, Gordon Wright, Robert Horn, and Paul Robinson. I hope my children are as blessed.

My other great teachers—John McPhee, Peter Drucker, William Zinsser, E. B. White, Theodore Levitt, John Tillman, Kurt Vonnegutt, Jr., Geoffrey Moore, Peter Senge, and Theodor Geisel—who taught me to write and changed the way I see.

The people at Stanford University in the early 1970s—particularly its generous Office of Admissions—who changed my life.

My friends—Wayne and Mary Dankert, Eleftheris and Jane Papageorgiou, Randy Vick, Peggy and Karl Weber, Steve Kaplan, Tom Cooper, Gary and Chris Cohen, Gregg and Tracey Kunz, Niki Koumas, Karl Larson, Cathy Madison, Joyce Agnew, Katie Barrett, Steve Schelhammer and Cathy Phillips—who encouraged me and make me feel lucky.

My second family—Judy and Joel Wethall, Barbara Wilson and John Lammers, Bob Wilson, Helen Wilson and Jane Hannan—because anyone who loves every moment he can spend with his in-laws truly *is* lucky.

My family—mother Alice, sister Becky, brother-in-law Jim Powell, and brother David Macy-Beckwith and his wife, Cindee—who cheered, laughed, loved, endured, and cooked meals about which even James Beard raved.

My heroes: Clive Davies, The Honorable James M. Burns, and Dr. Harry Beckwith, Jr.

My miracles: Harry, Will, Cole, and Cooper.

And my wife, Susan. I handled the writing but she did the heavy lifting—consulting and consoling and seeing me through. In my lucky life I have been blessed with four excellent models and a handful of miracles. Susan is both, and I am incredibly grateful.